To the Bone

To the Bone

NEW AND SELECTED POEMS

Sydney Lea

University of Illinois Press   URBANA AND CHICAGO

Manufactured in the United States of America
1 2 3 4 5 C P 5 4 3 2 1

This book is printed on acid-free paper.

Library of Congress Cataloging-in-Publication Data

Lea, Sydney, 1942–
     To the bone : new and selected poems / Sydney Lea.
          p.   cm.
     ISBN 0-252-02223-8 (cloth : alk. paper). — ISBN 0-252-06519-0
(pbk. : alk. paper)
     I. Title.
PS3562.E16T6   1996
811'.54—dc20   95-50189
                                                                       CIP

For my wife Robin

. . . How could he know you

would come, and come the day of which he sings?
Has gone on singing. Will go on to sing.

Contents

Acknowledgments

The author thanks the editors of the following periodicals in which certain of this volume's poems (occasionally in slightly different form) first appeared:

PART 1: *The Southern Review*: "Aubade," "Fourth of July"; *Wilderness*: "Hunter's Sabbath: Hippocratic"; *The New Yorker*: "Beautiful Miles," "November"; *The Michigan Quarterly Review*: "Athlete's Scars"; *Salmagundi*: "R.N., Women's Ward," "Peaceable Kingdom"; *The Missouri Review*: "Oosh"; *The Georgia Review*: "Valedictions," "To the Bone"; *The Virginia Quarterly Review*: "The Right Words in April," Mudtime in the County"; *The Connecticut Review*: "Friendship"

PART 2: *Ascent*: "Searching the Drowned Man: The Third Day"; *The Hudson Review*: "To the Summer Sweethearts," "For Don C., against a Proverb"; *Poetry Northwest*: "Night Patrol: The Ancestral House"; *The Southern Review*: "Elegy at Peter Dana Point," "Night Message for Ted in the South"; *The Sewanee Review*: "Drooge's Barn"; *The Beloit Poetry Journal*: "Band Concert"; *Prairie Schooner*: "Young Man Leaving Home"; *Texas Review*: "Night Trip across the Chesapeake and After," For My Son Creston at the Solstice," "The President of Flowers"; *The New Yorker*: "The Train Out"

PART 3: *The Iowa Review*: "To a Surgeon"; *The New Republic*: "A Natural Shame"; *The Ohio Review*: "There Should Have Been"; *The Kansas Quarterly*: "The Feud"; *The New Yorker*: "Accident," "The Floating Candles," "Bernie's Quick-Shave (1968)"

PART 4: *The Atlantic*: "Midway"; *The Georgia Review*: "Horn," "Tough End"; *The Kenyon Review*: "Annual Report"; *The New Republic*: "Making Sense," "Fall," "Sereno"; *The New Yorker*: "After Labor Day," "The Return: Intensive Care," "Leonora's Kitchen," "Dusk"; *The Partisan Review*: "The Light Going Down"; *The Virginia Quarterly Review*: "From Another Shore"; *Crazyhorse*: "No Sign"

PART 5: *The Laurel Review*: "Two Chets"; *Prairie Schooner*: "Pietà," "Late Season"; *Grand Street*: "Pianissimo"; *The New Yorker*: "Another Autumn, And"; *Antaeus*: "For Faith"; *The Partisan Review*: "Manifest"; *The Georgia Review*: "Museum"

PART 6: The Reaper: "The Blainville Testament"; *The Kenyon Review:* "Spite: Her Tale"; *The Laurel Review:* "Proem: After George's Ax Was Stolen"; *Crazyhorse:* "Private Boys' School, 3rd Grade"; *The Missouri Review:* "In the Blind"; *North by Northeast:* "Road Agent"; *Tar River Poetry:* "Black Bear Cuffing for Food"

. . .

Certain poems included here also appear in anthologies, to whose editors the author likewise expresses gratitude:

New York: Poems, ed. Howard Moss (New York: Avon, 1980): "Accident"; *Writing in a Nuclear Age,* ed. Jim Schley (Hanover, N.H.: University Press of New England, 1983): "After Labor Day"; *New American Poets of the 80's,* ed. Jack Myers and Roger Weingarten (Green Harbor, Maine: Wampeter Press, 1984): "A Natural Shame," "To the Summer Sweethearts," "After Labor Day," "The Return: Intensive Care"; *The Morrow Anthology of Younger American Poets,* ed. David Bottoms and Dave Smith (New York: Wm. Morrow, 1985): "The Train Out," "Night Trip across the Chesapeake and After," "Bernie's Quick-Shave (1968)," "The Floating Candles"; *The Bread Loaf Anthology of Contemporary American Poetry,* ed. Sydney Lea, Robert Pack, and Jay Parini (Hanover, N.H.: University Press of New England, 1985): "After Labor Day," "Sereno," "Fall"; *Strong Measures: Contemporary American Poetry in Traditional Forms,* ed. Philip Dacey and David Jauss (New York: Harper & Row, 1986): "There Should Have Been," "The Floating Candles"; *Keener Sounds: Selected Poems from* The Georgia Review, ed. Stephen Corey and Stanley Lindberg (Athens: University of Georgia Press, 1987): "Horn"; *Vital Signs: Contemporary American Poetry from the University Presses,* ed. Ronald Wallace (Madison: University of Wisconsin Press, 1989): "For My Father, Who Hunted"; *New American Poets of the 90's,* ed. Jack Myers and Roger Weingarten (Boston: David Godine, 1991): "Prayer for the Little City," "Museum"; *The Unfeigned Word: Fifteen Years of* New England Review, ed. T. R. Hummer and Devon Jersild (Hanover, N.H.: University Press of New England, 1993): "Wedding Anniversary"; *Poems for a Small Planet: Contemporary American Nature Poetry,* ed. Robert Pack and Jay Parini (Hanover, N.H.: University Press of New England, 1993): "The Fish Pond," "Paternity"; *Odd Angles of Heaven: Contemporary Poetry by People of Faith,* ed. David Craig and Janet McCann (Wheaton, Ill.: Harold Shaw Publishers, 1994): "Prayer for the Little City," "Road Agent," "Midway"; *Articulations: The Body and Illness in Poetry,* ed. Jon Mukand (Iowa City: University of Iowa Press, 1994): "To a Surgeon."

1

To the Bone

(1991–95)

To the Bone

In memory of Earl Bonness,
and for Susan Kennedy, R.N.,
who did the right thing

and I   I wanted too to do the right thing
for the woman whose husband had left her dirty
as hell   no car   no cash   two kids   no fuel
and wanted as well   it being Labor Day   to get it done and go home
wife   sons   daughters   the first tartness of autumn seeming
to tang the mist above our pond   and so I hurried

"up like a windowshade otherwise" said the surgeon
meaning what the quadricep sawn to the bone might've done
if Sue hadn't done   yes   the right thing and splinted and bound
my left leg so that the muscle would not   precisely
roll up that way   and what sort of god
has blessed me all my days that the nearest one

to me was one who knew what to do
which is not to mention that there were six stout men to bear me
from among those trees and down to where Marv and Louise
lived   and that   though it did plunge to   the blade did not plunge through
bone nor artery nor ligament nor center of inscrutable nerves nor tendon
and that the whole thing was so eerily

painless but for a moment
on the ER table when the intern
noting that the cut was a mess   decided to dress
the thing and shoved two packets of Betadined gauze to the bone
and I passed out and coming to heard somebody say *morphine*
which at first burned

and then through its haze the saw I saw took out my right bicuspid
porcelain crown and all and I watched the shards leap into woods
and there Earl Bonness stood   ancient   eloquent   understanding   good
Earl Bonness of Washington County Maine
who had known more pain than any intern could conjure
his girlchild   long since   at seventeen   having plain dropped dead

no one knew why   and one of his boys born with muscular dystrophy
and what of the grandson he and Tecky raised who raised a pistol and pointed
at the soft palate and felt of the trigger and pulled it
and here Earl scooched down to duck these tatters
of tooth that rattled into the woods
with a sound of rain   then he started

to speak as always he did because a story
gives shape to a life and I just let my brain drink it in like lifeblood
and   as to myself I always would say when I heard him say
a story   he spoke with the voice of many waters   old river-driver
it was good times you see but not all good

that river trip was a mighty tough job if I'm to be honest
we drove a billion board feet clear to the sea
and I woke because it was absurd that word
billion   but of course that was just morphine talking
not Earl who   as my wife would not tell me till a good while after
knowing the way I loved him   had died on the very day

of this wound   and the wound
being dirty as hell   I'd stay in the hospital five days hooked up
to the damned IV   all the while   needless to say
imagining Earl still alive   but just then   once I got past
the word *billion*   even if I knew it was closer to that
than to the measly six cord we meant to cut

for the abandoned woman   after I got past the billion I fell back in
and Earl recalled that *an old fella cooked for thirty-eight men on an open fire*
he had three cookees   helpers   which dried the pans and platters
by sticking them all in a flour sack and working them back and forth
by golly that cook was quite a man   I did like him
we worked all the daylight there were

and then Earl was gone
I did like them   those friends   and what would've happened otherwise
without the men and the woman who splinted and bound my big limb
with the trunk of a third-year maple
without which   as I was told on the steel
table   my wife beside me   and the drug seeming to make my very eyes

sweat as my brain went hot
what would've become of the muscle
yes   "up like a windowshade"   so I was more than glad
for morphine   less for killing pain than freeing me to think without muscle
and so to lapse under again
and hear Earl

say don't let me say there wan't ever no hard feelings of any kind
but a lot of them comical too   I'll tell a tale   a true one
we had us a boy back then in these parts   Jim Foy
he lived out on Tough End same as I do
and was he a character
and there'd come this peddler with a horse and wagon

about twice a month   Reuben the peddler
which had various things for sale on his cart but mainly clothes
and Reuben was up one evening at Grand Lake Landing
yes   a bright red evening time
when Jim and I come in from guiding
and pulled up our canoes

and Jim's pants being bedraggled somewhat he went over
to Reuben and said I need trousers
and they both sorted through till Jim Foy found a pair that'd do
we was paid five dollars a day as guides then
so when he asked of the peddler the price
and when he heard four dollars

why   Jim looked around and said god almighty for four dollars
I'd sell my moccasins   hat   shirt   everything I own
and Reuben just coughed   once   and then he said take 'em off
but how did this all come out I wondered as the last clap of tooth
sounded against the understory
all sweet fern and witch hazel frost-browned

by now   and the world   as after a beating   went silent
but for something that hummed outside the OR
did Jim get those trousers   I wondered   and wondered
whatever became of my own pants   irreparably rent
above the knee
the ones that should've been the pair

made of Kevlar that I'd looked at across the river
at Deb's Wheel & Deal the very day before   only to decide
not just then to buy because my own winter's supply
of cordwood was already bucked up
and all I needed
was to split the bigger chunks and stack the logs inside

and had only this little good deed to do with good people
and had cut about a billion board feet of wood with a power
saw in my   now   half a century   good God no
so was long on experience   *but there is always a trap*
set for you in the woods
or anywhere at all around lumber

said Earl   *one job I had was hanging boomstock*
for   you see   on the west river is many big flowage areas above the dam
at Grand Falls and they had to boom them logs off each and all
to keep them from getting in among the stumps
because it was so costly
to pull them out of there again

eighty bucks for the Kevlar trousers at Deb's
and I told her   well   another time
old Bill Park was the boss on the upriver work
and he said I don't know how you can do it
I was green
he said you walk clear out about to the end

of one of those sticks
then hop onto another and you ain't fallen in yet
I told him give me time and said it again   give me time
I was green
as I say   of course
I had a pair of good cog boots

6

made by the Bass Company   and still have them today in my shop
stepped over a lot of timber they did   you know
in all them days   but finally
but finally what   I don't know
well finally in came my children   or four of the five
the big one away at graduate school   good God no

and they looked at me funny
well likely I looked funny too   not funny ha-ha as my grandma used to say
but funny peculiar   forgive me   reader
if now I myself say
I didn't know whether to laugh or cry
I shouldn't put it so banally because I am supposed to have this way

with words but every time
push comes to shove   hate   love   joy   disease   trouble
words fail me   at least at first   as you can plainly
see and it's not a good feeling
it's like when I studied math in school
forever lost in the shuffle

but never mind math   never mind figures   it is hard
just to write your mind   and Earl to my mind was alive   who was ninety
who once told me   his old eye twinkly
that in the Depression *times got so bad and my deer dog so weak*
he had to lean agin a bank to howl
but in my dream he never finished the story

about hanging the boomstock by the dam
and although in this case my eyes were wide open
that dam appeared to me and I tell you it scared me
because what ran down through its sluice was water   yes
but also power-saw-dust
and human tooth upon tooth upon tooth for no good reason

and so I had to shut my eyes again to see again in mind
the true wound the chain gave me
which when it actually happened oddly first made me determined
to lose weight   there being a skim of fat over the muscle
as if what lay before me were in fact a roast
that needed maybe

7

ten minutes more in a three-fifty oven
I remember that cook   I did like him   Charlie Rogers
and next what I felt was rage that I should have reached
for the canted cherry log on the pile
and not taken time
not walked over

planted my feet and done the right thing as so often before
and thereby saved everybody   wife   friends   Susan
me   all this effort   anxiety   time   discomfort
and above all the children
and then for some reason mired as I was in cliché
I thought of that slogan

you see all over on the bumpers of the cars of the self-righteous
it shouldn't hurt to be a child
and   however cheap   the message made the most common but deep
deeper than that hell-dirty wound
sense to me there on the ward
where the device they wired into me was called

a morphine pump
which allows you to dose yourself at the push of a button
every sixth minute and each time you do it
you hear a little beep if you've waited long enough
on hearing which beep in one instance I beheld
as if from small distance   the teeth of a Pakistani music student

being washed down a gutter
after the boy had had his mouth placed on the curbstone
by the bald thugs   so vicious   diabolical   who had beaten him unconscious
there in the rain   until all had had their chance
had had a turn
at bringing cog boots down

on the back of his head
till he was dead
and in the article I read somewhere one of the attackers declared
it had been lots of fun but was over too soon
beep
falling under I wondered if that awful boy's mother still lived

8

and what she thought of such a son
and what she might have thought back when he was a child
before he could articulate any word much less one of hate
nigger   faggot   kike
o say did she hold him as one must
and did she try to sort out what his future held

to myself I say don't sentimentalize
because maybe the best she hoped for
was damn slight   I peeked for as long as I might
and there were four of my own blond lucky
babies   seventeen   ten   six   two
smiling at me and trying to look cheerful
because maybe the best she ever hoped for

was just something better than this
that dark melody- and harmony-loving boy and his teeth being rolled
by rude water   in some city she never saw   down a gutter
or something better than the life her husband had
working always but always worried that it would give out
this seam of east-slope Colorado coal

which would mean he'd have to find some other hole
somewhere   or else find something to grab onto aboveground
or maybe she simply yearned for her baby not at length to turn
suddenly surly to his woman after two or three weeks of hot constant sex
right after the wedding
but surely she never entertained

the notion that he'd be president
of anything   only   maybe   a straw boss hauling orange highway pylons
site to site in a pickup's bed   wearing a fedora on his head
or one of those bolo ties to seem like a big shot   and a clipboard on his dash
though who in hell did I think I was
I didn't have the slightest idea what she imagined

as for me   what I imagined next was a star that flared and went out
a ring nebula
and I too went out   but beforehand   I'm told   I gave a shout
and dropped again into a dream in which one of my brothers died
in a place to which I'd never been
called Tarquinia

and which   according to an Italian travel guide
I asked my wife on the phone to consult when I awoke and found her
gone   and also the children   as it seems they had been
for hours
I had not known them gone
and which place I found when I phoned her

was according to the guide
best known for its necropoli
and again   again   again   I pumped morphine
because the dream
had such an unaccountable grip
upon me   poor dead other Lea

even if in fact that brother had died   of stroke
back fourteen years
"rolled up like a windowshade" is what was said
dirty as hell
to the bone
tears

and then my wife and I decided on the phone not to tell my mother
about my wound   my mother
not being strong   having also had a stroke not so long
before and then her gut slit   crotch to sternum
and an aortal aneurism repaired
then someone entered

who was and is now a blur
a woman I think   and said *it has been a bad year*
why am I always so slow to recognize what's before my eyes
through the almost palpable aura on my skin
I could feel the wet of my weeping
and thought   yes   dirty as hell   yes   a bad year

there having for example been once a boy by the name of Whitman
my absent oldest boy's best chum when they were children
than whom I verily say unto you and it's true
was never more beautiful a child
who got into booze
when he was an adolescent

then into crack cocaine
and who in the May past had hanged himself   and my big son
spoke a eulogy so lovely it damn near killed me
about how Breck once "made us see with new and better eyes"
and I pray it's also true the least sparrow
is somewhere counted   for beside young Whitman

I will speak of George Lawson
who after a certain fellow left his garage
the one with the big   old   fine   red-wing horse on its sign
asked me if I knew the man and what he did and I told him
and George said   o   yeah   a poet   he LOOKED like a fuckin' poet
upon which I pledged

I'd myself get George himself into a poem and George told me
no you can't   but here I can   now that he's gone
for all the good it can do   for George who felt like family too
and dropped from heart failure
into the arms of my friend Terry
who was and is his son

all these tatters   none of which is even to mention   a Rwanda   a Bosnia
nor an eleven-year-old I read of in Time who killed somebody
and then got killed too because his gang was afraid he knew
too much   his nickname
this much I recall
was Yummy

and how's that for how it shouldn't hurt to be a child
Yummy knew too much
and I not one fucking fact   well   no   I wouldn't say that
because there was more
than ever one fact now I sure to God knew
and yet do   which was this   that the flesh

was fragile the world over   as for example that of my wife's father
dead by cancer   and of her brother
the cop who was just fine by now but who had once cropped
a toe half off with a power mower which made him
I smiled it struck me with such odd delight   because I loved him
one who'd been shot at   a sort of blood brother

11

but I saw blood on the dam
tooth toe and bullet   now   uncannily   floating in it   beep said the pump
and so I considered what is leached from a woman or man whenever
the blood runs out
and meat goes cold
and organs slump

viz.   as much as body parts
all the songs one ever learned
which would have to include in my case for the most part blues
to which by birth I have of course no right
but let the right person   ordinarily of African descent
but sometimes white   bend

those same old twelve bars and that same old bunch
of one and four and tonic chords   the flatted third and seventh notes
as the good ones forevermore can   and my body takes it all in
to the bone   and now I remembered
across long distance
across three decades   in a club choked with smoke

Muddy singing   exactly   *Long Distance Call*
about picking up the telephone
and someone telling him *another mule is kickin' in your stall*
great God   what a figure
and there were at least two things that I wanted
very much to know back then

first why that line was not as good as some of Dante's or Homer's
and second why the twelve bars
were not as surprising as sonata form or at least   as those three closing
chords you hear in every damn nineteenth-century symphony
and here now are the answers
o it was   o they were

and I woke and wondered how did I get here
o yes   I'd been thinking of the things that are leached and lost
when the eyes fall shut and heart flickers out
well   I supposed   that depends
on who one is or thinks s/he is
in my case death shall cost

no less than the memory of my breathtaking wife
memory that   forgive my triteness   just sticks in the mind
against the sky at the height of a certain obscure small mountain
devoid of trails
hidden therefore   we were more thrillingly than ever alone
a place that   in accord with Mark   only the right ones can find

(a nod to Frost here)
a certain indigo bunting in Dean Pushee's unkempt hedge
and a certain black-phase rough-leg hawk and a half-dozen high-head dogs
wild columbine and painted trillium and my heart-filling children
a small bear cuffing for ants on the Woodsville road
Don Chambers hitching his great Belgian mare Queenie to a sledge

none of which
you have the least awareness of   and why on earth
reader   why on earth should you   no   I'm speaking rather
of the sorts of signs that any body gathers
in the lifelong effort to make a life cohere
and give it worth

and I have small doubt
your signs are other far
and yet do you not swear   then doubt yourself   then again swear
as the night air bears upon you
the sounds outside   such as they are wherever you are
oppressive   it all comes together somewhere

o beautiful suicide boy   o Breck Whitman   o George Lawson
and other dead loved ones   o father   o brother   o Earl   and so on
and o flowers even   and birds   and o good dogs   and words
and though the wound in the leg
proved dirty as hell
it was less long than it might have been

before I was out of the hospital
thanks to Susan and my wife and friends   it all flows together somewhere
or else it doesn't but floods out   and spends itself into loss   absolute
and days passing ponderously
and nights too bed-bound as I was   and no more drugs
I would lie there and ponder

until   on a certain midnight
my family asleep above me like angels
like angels supervening   yes   I lay half-dreaming
and once again wondered
what is the chain
and did I hit on that figure because a chain wandered at a blood-chilling angle

to the bone   I don't know
I account for nothing   but now the blood didn't chill and didn't cascade
as it had along with the rest of that visionary mess
that detritus sluiced down the dam for days
for there was no longer a dam   I wish I could tell you why and tell myself
it was just that this was healing   which is not to say

that Earl rose before me in his flesh   new flesh   fragile flesh
nor that I knew death   dirty as hell   to have no dominion
nor that I could stand at last   as in some bad movie   and cast
crutches away   nor that I could retrieve   for instance
brother or father   nor that by mere will I could mend my mother
they were still absent   Lawson and Whitman

but is to say that all these again were things that I just might
imagine   the wound sealing itself such that again I'd refer to me
as a being entire   and such that this ceaseless current bearing every desire
we name it life   would come out all right
it would be all right   it would be all right
whatever it might be

28 September–11 October 1994

14

Hunter's Sabbath: Hippocratic

the gauzy lichen here
to mask this granite
I know I will not save
invading
as often will be hare's
and cat's
thin trail out
that I may leave
than they incise
in easy passing
nor greater wound
in any less than
today I will not prey
my way may do
but let it do at least

took years
patient earth
nor cure
yet today my path
and deer's
described by scat and track
thin trail back
no greater scar
on scarp and peak
unpursued
than weather makes
fevered mood
nor storm
no earthly good
no harm

The Right Words in April

I stay in the present even though it's many years ago that I ask the woman
to name her hair's odd color   Now it's now   the future   & I can't recall her
description   She's a girl really even if I say *woman*   & I'm a boy at a party
down in Richmond Virginia   Who in the world throws it & why I'm invited
I'll die before I can say   Yet today   or actually yesterday   time evaporates
or partway   I stroke our baby's hair in wooziest devotion   hair of a shade
so alike it puts all these notions in motion   She sits in her infant seat amid
cookiecrumbs appleskins   et cetera   as we drive to school to fetch her sister
I can't for my life fetch up the other   her face or name or how she calls her
hair or why a bit of it seems so crucial   Copious sap runs into the maples
In brooks ice breaks   Ice broken some sparks do fly but all we do by & by
is smalltalk   (& the last time we'll meet is this day)   though big things brew
already in Alabam'   She pronounces it so   as if in mockery of her own sort
of speech   & of course Viet Nam   That much I can report   & her bleached
eyes' color   also unusual   even if I'm not ready to judge whether beautiful
& I can see a scar   It stands out on the tan skin of her arm white as a star
She says it was made by a brother   He stabbed her in a temper tantrum
so hard with scissors she bled   no matter they were a round kindergarten
kind   He meant to cut off her head   Maybe   I think   smartass kid   he did
She hefts the hair as if it were bloody   1959   September   month when Joe
a neighbor's son   dies in a fire in the peacetime navy   or maybe a barfight
I don't remember   & don't remember the girl's name in Virginia that night
& how she describes her hair   But why do these matter anyway compared
to real matters   to all those people burned away   say   down in Waco Texas
where some died right off & later many   all on account of religious zealots
It's only that I want   what   the personal   even the daily   even the trivial
still to count   & to see 30 years as other than a blur   Trying at all events
to summon a name & word   I stray across a white line   & look up in time
to see my own death   Some will claim when you whiff that hot salt breath
your life on earth passes before your eyes   & for what it's worth I'll testify
o yes that's true   at least parts do   but I can't even tell which ones as now

I yank my wheel back toward the right ditch   & we sway   & lean   & lurch
& the baby cries   & before my eyes is the great grille's tin grin   & then
in the truck's bed   logs & a cherrypicker crane   & sky above   I'll be dead
soon   It seems incredibly sad   because   unlike some   I have always loved
being husband & being father   Yet of course for our baby it is even sadder
so pink   her time on earth so small   But now the airhorn blasts   o glory be
behind me   & life is rich   & so after all   I think   I'll see everyone again
& so I breathe at last   *oh yes   it was Butterscotch   &   oh yes   Mary Jane*

Peaceable Kingdom

Heedless, the ruffian hills have smirched their bibs with claret.
There, the roof of a playhouse dries, seeps, dries.
If nature and weather own rhetoric, it is their own;
If these birds will tell us nothing of surer climates
Than this, taking the skies;
If we can't know whether thought's involved in the insects' cocoons;
Can there still be one who, stubborn, might render
Everything here in the mode of naïve painters?—
Each beast at peace, and so on.

It is no single sadness he'd have to transform, repress,
But all of them: We may know of a mourned-for child, for instance,
Who'd made her parents and others fret and smile
By means of her inconsequential syntax.
He'd have to ignore resistance,
Let her drift in cloud, although the fact is that she fell
Like so many. Even the playhouse withers.
The scenes he'd use she never saw, nor the weathers
In which he'd trick his smoothing tales,

Nor his patterns, legends—Those beasts at peace, great and tiny;
Trees canted low with mast for the ones of grander size,
With plenteous seed and sap for bird and squirrel;
At the river surface, shiny
Fish that rise but merely kiss the flies;
He'd try to envision such contexts not just for the single girl:
Who else may go or has gone under?
Wind and frost are eloquent of their number.
That's the trouble with the world.

That's what he'd hope to limit for us, the random expense.
He labors to figure a final soft drift through
A whisper of sky and into what he sketches,
To purge the freeze, the gale. Inconsequence:
At once his Terror, Muse.
Can he really call it *gentle fire*, that underedge
Of the livid clouds of the coming downpour,
Or really name it *bark* or *winged car*—
That child's sad, plain bed,

Or anyone's—as skies explode in middle sentence?
As fish burrow down in mud; as night birds whoop, stammer;
As silk-clenched moths impound their own mute glamour.
O, inconsequence, inconsequence . . .
Hardened, the puddles' shores,
And jagged; animals correct his sought-for grammar.
Heedless, he may yet speak of rest,
May give us certain scenes, and souls, and lore,
Though November's heavens thunder past.

Mudtime in the County

His old man's gone under the ground, who bruised him black when young.
So has the drunken uncle whom people nicknamed Coal-chunk,
who hurt him otherwise, who's likely dead as well,
though how say how or where? Violently in jail
would make a decent bet, or in a ditch at nightfall,
some other savaged boy, grown at long last manful,
turning tables. This fellow Ron—I've heard him called

the homeliest child who ever crowned at birth—now crawls
in four-wheel-drive along these battered roads to gather
trash, litter. Dumpman, living like his father:
Load. Unload. Pick over. Again. Again. Again.
Each day the three trips forth and back to Bethlehem,
our place for rubbish, waste. Yet everything's reversed.
I've heard her named the coarsest woman treading earth;

her name and his, however, make internal rhyme:
RON & RHONDA, block print wrought in neon lime
adhesive tape, and they have shaped the letters backward
on the grille. Their signs read forthright in my mirror.
I look back. They shine. They huddle close as bugs.
I see them share their Lucky Strike and warm noon Bud
and dark-tooth sighs, and up ahead and on each side

a world whose beauties had grown tedious, old, and died
reverts to charm. Is it mere dream, that gleam in mud
the woodchuck hurled up, heroic, as she dug
her brood den's pitch-black chambers? Fieldmouse tracks and rats'
pursue each other over ditch and shoulder, back
and forth, while from a blighted pinecrown, grim as coal,
a woodpecker showers down its lode of square-wrought gold.

Beautiful Miles

Thunder outdoors.
He stacks shelves, though his children's dishes file in as if by themselves:
        A pair of plates just there,
        Six gaudy tumblers directly under,
So the baby daughter's safety cup is crowded.
        There's something about it
        —The household's loose order—that generally reassures,
        And the storm's still far.

        One's life, dear clutter
Assumed across the years. *Me* become *Mine*, *Us* become *Ours*.
        Here is another, older
        Girl's bowl that she made in school,
3rd grade. Pastiche of colors, a serpent
        Turns a circuit,
        Begins as gold, goes black around the border.
        Her father considers

        Beautiful miles,
Their puzzling splendors: for instance how he and his two little brothers
        Would kneel by that tall pile
        Of swimming hole rocks, in one of whose clefts
A snake always lisped, jetting its feces. They reeked.
        A single peek,
        And the younger boys thought, This is danger. But each a child,
        Each smiled.

        Stink and sweat.
Rough nap of his towel. Minor quake of lightning down in his bowels
        As he probed the crack with a stick.
        Half-cruel, he smiled at the snake's recoil

Deeper into the fissure, and at the look of the brothers
—Pleasure in terror:
They were grinning but chilled, despite the sun on their backs.
But what has all that

To do with a fool
In the dark, with his banal works? He knows. He goes on loading the racks
While freakish weather fills
The winter sky. A fool could say why
—Here in predawn January, sleepless—
He fools with these dishes.
The china serpent lips its golden tail.
The bowl is so frail.

He loves his life.
He loves the beautiful miles, for all the crudeness of their details:
This saucer, this blunt-tipped knife,
These cratered spoons and sheltering rooms,
And above all, above him, the quick and dead who've loved him
And continue to move him:
Parent. Son. Daughter. Sibling. Wife.
There will come strife,

One must assume.
Clumsy, the painted snake's eye; and yet less clumsy, he thinks, than I,
Mine. The lightning again.
Oil roars in the furnace. Too many near misses,
And worse. In those miles one has to envision great damage,
For example the hemorrhage
That assaulted one of the brothers, reduced him to stone.
One assumes pain.

Yet the lovely distance:
He'd travel every inch again, in company with them . . .
Back to his silly business.
Back in thunder to the familiar.
Back to his station, to resisting a sort of invasion
Of nameless legions,
Though in fact there can never quite be sufficient resistance,
Assuming a conscience.

Soldiers in bunkers
Pass orders in fearful hisses. Another chain-bolt sizzles and flashes.
There are planes on ships on the waters.
What is his right to guilt or fright?
None, unless it be imagination's,
Assumed in migration
Over its miles, storm grown ever louder,
Ever closer.

Fourth of July

The American flag was the last thing to burn,
in whose glare every last face looked white. And *was*,
except for the Guatemalan's.
I learned he was Guatemalan because I eavesdropped.

Part of an infinitesimal middle class,
he'd come for some multinational conglomerate's training
program, held at a famous college a short trip down to the south.
His face had color; all others were white as I say, and each looked healthy.

Beautiful: the fireworks doubling themselves in the lake all evening,
and people—though it wouldn't be right
to call any one of them wealthy—appeared to be doing just fine.
Me too. And yet, as Wordsworth once put it,

"As it sometimes chanceth, from the might
Of joy in minds that can no further go,
As high as we have mounted in delight
In our dejection do we sink as low." Not that I'd felt joy, not exactly,

nor that I now felt exactly dejection. And it had nothing to do
with *might*, whatever it was I was feeling—or at least not my own.
Or at least I wouldn't have thought so. But be all that
as it may, there surely enough did seem to be a certain direction

in which my mind
could not keep on mounting. And as it wound down,
or fell, or turned, or whatever it did, a voice said, "Let me hold a dime."
And another one said, "Let me cut him, King."

This was memory—in which the first voice spoke again:
"Fact, little brother, let me hold *all* your dimes."
On that beach the men behind these words took shape in sudden vision,
dressed in their sharp-creased double-breasted suits, hair conked

and shiny with bergamot in the manner of the times,
three decades gone.
So forget Wordsworth or anyone else I then studied
at the famous college to southward,

because one of these guys longed to cut me, longed to get it done
and ask somebody else for coins later;
but it was the other one who had the say,
in part because his friend with the knife was so drunk, near knee-walking.

The Kennedy era, this was, when things kept getting better,
so we imagined. And so I kept wanting to get a say, too — something
about a new day dawning, maybe, or I hoped so, really,
but something too about not in fact being

anyone's little brother but the oldest sibling
of five: three boys, two girls, all still alive that night.
I must have imagined a rightness,
a vague sort of benevolent order.

Sure, I had it all wrong about what seemed right.
I was likely, and may still be, wrong about every last earthly matter,
and in my error, under those wheezing streetlamps,
I strangely envisioned late dusk at my uncle's farm,

and — their dark bodies uncertainly doubled by water —
his tame ducks vanishing in the last shadows, where willows bent,
which memory of the tranquil
somehow meant I deserved neither robbing nor stabbing,

a silly thing for me to have thought it meant,
though maybe no sillier than for this man, however imposing,
to call me *little*, since I wasn't.
Up to the moment when the flag exploded

at the closing,
the fireworks had been pretty tame, and that seemed good.
Good, the almost pastoral, evening-star glitter
of lesser bombs, damped *thumps* of their reports, whiffs of cordite,

and the cooled debris raining harmless among us where we stood,
I and my wife
and our smaller children, for whom the finale
would soon prove mildly disruptive,

or do I here speak only of my own little life?
In any case, I recalled that man from that time named King,
not Martin Luther, as for the love of me and nation I should have done,
but him who reduced me to nothing, the pomaded one

who caught me crosstown, just looking
to hear some music, good music—twelve bars, backbeat, riff and slide—
that was a far cry from the oom-pah stuff
from the gazebo on the common the afternoon before this fireworks show.

And once I'd brought this bullying son of a bitch to mind,
I kept at it, recalling every insult or slight,
and every last thing that force of will could make seem so,
though such old resentment had never done me much good,

even when I came out clean. Seeing the weak-rayed LITE
and BUD signs in the window of a roadhouse, for instance, I'd turned
on a more recent evening and driven into the lot
and sat in the car and studied the Harleys lined up in a gleaming row

while something burned
in my scalp and my gut. And even though my 50th year had gone by,
I wondered if I might, just might,
be king of this shitty little hill for a little while,

and was just about ready to step inside
when out came some bald old boy with his own gut hanging,
and lit by the feeble throbs of the neon,
his eyes seemed almost entirely empty, entirely white,

mouth set in some expression of yearning,
fingers crankcase greasy, and I thought, He's seen the things I've seen
but still—after all these years—
can't understand. Or maybe I've never seen them at all.

Slowly he weaved away on his stupid fat machine,
I put my key back in, the new engine purred,
tires chirped.
And here now this Guatemalan, so quiet, so polite:

what his nation needed—as I heard
him say to someone because I eavesdropped—had less to do
with politics exactly than with what he quaintly named "civilization."
He spoke of soccer riots, corruption, terror, mayhem in the streets.

"How different it is with *you*,"
he whispered, eyeing the crowd on the beach, and out on the lake,
the moored boats, from which small talk was murmurous
above tinkles of ice between soft salvos.

"I ain't got no problem, fer Chrissake!
I didn't go to no fuckin' college!"
On the day I'd heard this—'64, summer job, Colorado—
I didn't know thing one about class, in America or anywhere,

and thus empowered by my terrible absence of knowledge,
I backed him down, that aging construction stiff, because he'd lit
himself up in rage against me, rage that struck me
as unaccountable, because I was bigger,

and anyhow, what had I done? As I say, I knew jack shit.
Then we went back building road. Kids, our own and others,
looked so damned cute and blond,
tiny round butts denting their blankets into the sand.

As they clutched spent sparklers,
their eyes were round too, and their flesh—in the old saw's words—
looked good enough to eat,
though no one ate flesh,

not that sort,
but rather plain old American hot dogs washed down by ginger ale,
while the languid roman candles,
the small-town rockets,

the half-functional Catherine Wheel
fizzed and flared, and the lake showed each back at itself.
And in the end, as the flag flamed
and the biggest blasts the fire department could afford boomed,

whatever it was that I felt
—not quite dejection—almost fell away,
almost became joy, as I thought, My son Jordan loves his daddy,
and his daddy loves him and everyone,

and maybe after all this hasn't been such a bad day.
In fact our little Catherine said that of all holidays this was the best one,
that she loved Mommy and Nana, all the family,
and she said, *Happy everything to everybody,*

and told how she missed her big brother Creston,
who was away, and worked her way into the lap of big sister Erika
as the last of it guttered in water
and people rose up, and the quiet Guatemalan uttered

Happy America.

Oosh

Why is the land ruined
and laid waste like a wilderness . . . ?
   —Jeremiah 9:10

What was it that he voiced? Perhaps the rush
of sustenance he felt and *heard.* That *oosh:*
until his first full year of life elapsed,
the nonce-word, nonce-sound, nonsense brought the breast.
In any hour. He had only to decide
to draw the shirt or shawl or blouse aside.

Oosh. To say it also meant to be
just where he meant to be. And equally
we're jaunty when the pleasurable obtains
in things we need to do, in the routine:
come Sunday, reeking garbage cans to load,
I find I all but dance out on my toes
to drive to the dump, where I am sure to find,
as I expect, the same old neighbors, friends.

We group and gaze into the barrel fire
that Charlie's lit. (We call him "Mr. Mayor,"
benign custodian of the dump, because
of all our townsfolk he's most recognized . . .)
Weather, town, and team, just this and that:
a tribe, it seems, we stamp our feet and chat
a while, and then disperse into our lives.
Fathers, husbands, mothers, children, wives.

It's nothing, yes. Yet I at times imagine
those lives without it somehow might be barren.
For all that we are cruel, or may be so,
wracked by sickness, anger, bills or woe,
for all that winter's bleakest woods surround us,
we're all sustained here by our idle sounds.

For all that we may wander or may suffer,
in this our weekly moment we're together.
You know it's silly, yes, but in your way
know what I mean, I'm sure. In our own ways,
we're sure sometimes. And so in that first year
his idle word, his less than word, was sure

and buoyant as our dump talk. *Oosh,* he'd say,
as some of us might say, "Give us this day—"
in a Sunday when in fact all our desires
seem ready to be met: crisp autumn air
and dazzling trees, the game on television.
Now he says it—*oosh*—but it is different.

I loom here in the darkness. *Oosh.* He shudders.
He knows the word for milk, and he knows others.
And yet through all these hours he's being weaned
he'll cling to it for life, his magic sound
that works no magic now, and so is thick
with pain and wonder: *Mother, I am sick.*

Dear Mother: Oosh! I'm sick at heart. I'm crazy.
Here are the desert ruins, Mother. Save me.
Mother of God, have you dispatched this demon?
Must I wander, Mother, the fallen nation,
wearing my threadbare beggar's blanket, lost?
Oosh, dear Mother! Rock me on your breast.

Aubade

Dressed up and not looking half bad if I say so
I saw Ilona because it was sunny that day
In her dull dress in springtime in her yard by my tram stop
In Budapest and every last tree in town in bloom tra-la-la
And she was big as a tree herself but didn't bloom
Yet pretty soon clickety clickety clickety the little yellow

Trolley'd come and off to work I'd go
While Ilona stood and looked at some keys she held up over her head
And turned them in her grasp and hummed
Which because she couldn't talk may have signaled some emotion
Or desire who knows not me
Who was only a professor of literature hired

For six months to teach what's called a survey
And this morning I would talk about *The Yellow Wallpaper*
Which is a hard book to talk about for a man
Or for anyone but I didn't feel nervous
Or worried having my lecture notes which were terribly thorough
Right in my old kit bag and just now somehow

The Yellow Wallpaper seemed more like a play anyway
And those keys like the big old kind you might see in a play
Or maybe a slapstick movie and their metal caught the air's dazzle
Winkety wink and her mother sat on some mealy steps
Strong enough or was it depressed
After so many years as not to be embarrassed

Nor even to notice
The American visitor who lived for now on the better
Side of her street and would soon go home

While her daughter's mouth kept clamping on its own rough growl
Mm mm mm so that the strange longbow set of the lips
Looked like part of a cartoon called *Hungarian Girl*

And birdies were there and viburnum and exquisite essence
Of lilac while her sausagey feet
Mashed the mud near the Soviet factory house so carelessly
Slapped up I could actually watch the progress of its ruin
Toward pure evanescence
And with housing scarce already what will become of

Many people when ashes ashes they all fall down
And of Ilona who'll never even be able
To work across the gray Danube at brand new awful McDonald's
And in the garden behind our nice apartment
O hell just like in Wordsworth was a small green swell of earth
Under which lay our beautiful neighbor

Judit's beautiful cousin who'd come up out of his cellar
And swallowed a slug in the siege
And no one knows if the gun was German or Russian
And I thought come on tram because sunlight kept pouring down
As though from some chemical weapon
And L.A. kindled as Ilona fiddled with some idiot keys

And skinheads did in some gypsies in Pest
And stooges some African township
And all the cordite and smoke from everywhere lifted and drifted
Under the hole in the ozone
Where cancers conspire
And then regathered and then slammed

Lead like a safe in Laurel and Hardy on Sarajevo
While people hid in their bunkers
While Ilona the big the fat the repulsive the mad
Kept revolving the keys in her cauliflower clump of a hand
As if she might choose one hey nonny and stick it in some big lock
Which would squeal and rattle

And puff out a fine orange rain of rust o o o
As a gate swung open to let her go
Into this
Unamendable wide waste fucking world
And I thought well then maybe ignorance is bliss
And I ought to know

Valedictions

For Erika, and for George

So much supplanted here in so few years,
ancient-rooted families almost gone.
Dear daughter, though the M.B.A. and lawyer
supervene, as we did once, this dawn
I think of our dead neighbor George, who loved you,
who for this day, your grade school graduation,
once pledged to bring you something from his garden.
One big smelly rose. That's what he vowed.
His plot is osier, joe-pye, purslane, rue.
Whatever else, there will be sense in heaven.
Why'd you think my family all was Beans?
His smile was true. *God meant us to be growers.*

He blessed you from your birth, plump bud of life.
Nose pressed against your pale pink crown, he swore,
She's sweeter than them godforsaken flowers,
and rocked you underneath his honey locust,
although his chest, more than the leaves, made shade.
He knew your little girlhood, and your passion—
at once adult and childish—for a radish
washed down by gulps of icy ginger ale;
and later saw the hairdos—pixie, page boy,
the one you tried to ape from Crystal Gayle,
that country-western singer he adored.
He praised them all, each more than those before.

He'd always be, you said, your only boyfriend,
and yet he watched you bloom just ten short years,

before these later boys imagined beards.
An imitation barn across his lane
has cropped up lately in what had been meadow,
no rank beast within, but fake-quaint toys.
("Authentic," so they're labeled, though to what
authority they owe themselves is moot.
They stink, I think.) For toy you had his tractor.
You'd bounce before him on its springless seat,
his hairy, muscled arm wreathed tight around you—
arm withered soon, untimely, cancer-slack.

Untimely, too, just now to maunder over
Time. But if he saw you! Tall and slim.
These other changes, though, he would have loathed:
they do not graduate; they bolt like weeds,
like farm kids bolted off to different places,
who keep the grounds of hospital or college,
or tend new lawns, or mind the marble orchards.
Yet if I let myself unwish too much,
I'd unwish you, as George would never do.
With time you will arrive at your own knowledge,
bittersweet like mine, perhaps. Forgive
my pseudo-Georgic reminiscence here,

accepting what George had of joy, alive,
and what I have as well, although his world
grows like you away with every season.
Let earth go on, I pray, and keep forever
whatever elementary things it needs:
some sweetness to perfume the summer air,
a field or two of hay to dream up seed,
moon to rise above his hill, and sun
to make a day like this one, red and new.
May all days be so bright. Now take this one
big smelly rose. It is not for his grave
but for your hair, all redolent of you.

Wear it for the sake of his dear shade.

The Fish Pond

No matter the name, it isn't full of fish,
but full it is, too full: frogs, crawdads, backswimmers, newts—
        prolix, little, dull.
Yet they were what drew to the scummed September surface
a single-minded osprey. *Acute*, he thought;
        that's the word. As claws pierced water and wings shone wet,
his vision of his own life's purpose
looked fragmentary, qualified,
        jerry-rigged with age like anybody's:
worse than mere impediment,
beneath contempt.
        He's always been moved by raptors in their dives,

figures from his long, long dream to strike directly.
Moribund, the broadleaves soon will drop.
        When school let out, his children dropped
their books in the mudroom's clutter:
ball gloves, rucksacks, dander on the tile.
        A local public official's smile
smeared the first page of the evening paper.
Though many loves live blessedly
        at home, he came away alone, out here.
And yet how quickly everything returns to trivial:
the pond—again, already—a turmoil
        of squirming things; and somehow riled,

pods of touch-me-not exploding on the shore,
spilling their countless seed.
        Hard to bear in mind, a bird,
its solitary shriek and plunge, its grip.

He kneels down on the strip of gravel beach to plead,
        vaguely, quaintly, upward. Hear me. Hear.
But is it *to* or is it *from* some one
that he wishes a word?
        It seemed the fish hawk knew to prey
and rise at once, to slip
not out of sight alone
        but even sound: two mongrels yip

in someone's dooryard, north, close by;
there's hissing homebound traffic southward;
        elsewhere, degenerate clamor
of fattening hens and geese as dusk sneaks east.
He's bound to all this by nature, sense —
        sand damp on his sore knees, a huff of breeze
pawing his neck and bearing further scents
of surfeit: moldered hay,
        grainfields' cloying germ and ear and tassle,
methane, deadfall, mossy stones
honed to myriad forms
        by streams from five surrounding swamps,

their weed- and root-growth thick as hair on cattle.
Now smaller beasts inside their warrens
        prepare for random ambulations,
crepuscular and timid: worthy victims,
each beneath consideration . . . though what is *he*?
        What sort of man would kneel these hours away
in his longing to strike or to be stricken?
All is imprecision. Hear, oh hear, he mumbles,
        while a corn moon stains the hundred humpback mountains,
a thousand shadows clog the meadow,
a million beings stir,
        and stars in pale herds mill in the very sky

where dully he beheld that sharp hawk on the air.

November

Mack's insides still ached from the test
at the fancy new clinic. The pain bothered less, though,
than how he'd had to lie there like that—Lord!—rear up,
and even the nurses watching. Almost to home now,

he saw Riddle's herd, the lot of them lying down on the ground.
Everything pretty and sad: the Holsteins'
black and white that bold and true, and after a rain-day or two,
the grass—more than in summer—that green.

The mountainsides showed their trees shaved clean,
except for the dark of the oak and the beech leaves, over the river,
fog on the bald ridges awful, the white of ice. Already.
Not cancer.

He ought to be relieved, said the doctors.
They only found some little thumbs—a five-dollar word he forgot
the minute they named it—on the bowel wall.
Not uncommon, they called it. Like death, Mack thought.

He passed the school. Everyone up on the swings or on foot:
Tag. Football. Capture the flag. The kids
still looked like October in all their bright clothes.
They raced as if wind-chased, fast as he drove. So this wasn't it.

Not the six dragged-out months that his young wife got,
and not a shock, either, like their one child Thelma's accident.
He was all right, but he'd die.
You know that the whole while, but then one day it's different,

like going by Fifth Mile Meadow and now there's a house built in it,
or a restaurant you dress up for where Joey Binder's mill was.
Mack determined not to get going on that. Not again.
He'd turn up his hill, check his mailbox,

maybe come back and *fix* the foolish mailbox,
about to lie down on its side. He'd check in on his tiny string
of heifers. Instead he held steady, north.
Watson claimed he'd got out of dairy for good, just barbering

full-time in his little shop in the yellow frame building
across from the feed store: it hadn't changed much, if at all.
"Say that for the rest," Mack whispered. "Say that."
And their talk hadn't changed. Animals, crops. But before Watson could pull

the paper ring from around his neck, Mack spoke: "Well,
I'll have a shave." How did it happen? It felt like dreaming.
"Yes, I guess I'll have a shave," he decided.
And then, the cloth on his face steaming

while his friend gripped the ivory handle in his big fingers, stropping
the blade on dirt-dark leather, Mack said
through the fog, "I haven't had this done in years. Years."
But it felt good. Lord, it did feel good!

Paternity

He waves his breakfast knife and screams he'll kill me.
Old mitigations—
he's hungry, tired, his pain and fury

have nothing to do
with me, will pass into nothing—
pass into nothing, my flight to reason

failing against these morning shrieks
that augur murder.
He slams the door, the very lath of the ceiling

quakes, and a precious print that now means nothing
tilts on its tack. The boy is my son.
The print is a Hopper,

Night Shadows: a man
crossing from dark to dark through uncertain light,
unspeakably alone.

The boy has hiked his socks, his short pants sag,
so that only the cap
of his knee still shows, abraded by play, or might

still show if he'd stayed.
The knee becomes a pink epitome
of all I desire: dumb, rapt,

I stare at a door.
And then, *tweet-tweet,* I imitate the birds
outside, that the child may hear and judge me

not indifferent, but not inclined
(though it's a lie)
to overvalue the stab of impassioned words.

I whistle to be
translated—that suddenly seeming the burden
of life, long life, damned long life—

and to show another side. Let him assume
again my mind,
like my flesh and blood, I think, as equally sudden,

coffee water leaps from spout to burner,
its mists and hisses
portending the inner clouds and windy sounds

of a place where I'll fall
and be flogged by the wing of doubt, by dream's wing,
and predatory Eros's.

I *will* the fall,
as one might choose to welcome the coming of migraine:
better than nothing, that chill in the skin

of the left-hand thumb,
the numbing tongue, the shadow sight,
twitch of nerve and muscle along the jawline.

Now something flashes
upon that inward eye that is the horror
of solitude: only a silly bike,

its Reelfur coontails flapping from handgrips,
and I astride.
A door has banged. Behind me, the calls of my father,

then tuneless whistles. Starling. Cowbird. Jay.
There's a shadow or fog
ahead, toward which I glide:

cloud in which our earthly cries must end,
I think, and think,
Damned short as well as long.

I want to fly back,
to the cup we bought for a joke at that tourist trap
with its sunrise scene, calm, pink

flamingoes wading through its maudlin inscription;
coffee; a household, sweet, foursquare;
belled cat on the lip

of the worn-wood kitchen counter, yawning;
the woman who for all our parenthood
lies ripe as pears

in autumn, stored behind closed doors.
I long to lay a soothing
hand on the blood-

and grass-stained knee of the boy
who chokes and sobs.
And so in my need to conjure something

against the fog, I summon the image
of a mourning dove
who flies backlit in mind across

the sun, is dark,
a dagger: a side, I'll say, of peace.
Dark dagger, but still a dove.

Peace, or its winged partner, love.

Friendship

For Joe Olsen

It was a Sunday. As usual you were working overtime. And I
as usual under. I: questions, remarks—windy, inane. You:
grunts between beats of your hammer. Suddenly you looked
up, as if shocked, like a man who's surprised by a mirror.
The bird had lit. Like your tool, it was poised, the great
wedge of a head. "Woodpecker," you said, your voice flatter
than clapboard. You repeated the word, this time a whisper.
It was the pileated: not uncommon. We'd seen such a bird
before, in fact in plenty. But in clutching its pine this one
spoke from prehistory. No, maybe it didn't.

        More than likely, this is only
sentimentality. The pine had been marked by a logger.
Loggers, carpenters—conspirators. And I as well, who dwell
indoors. So it would go down in time, that tree—to boards.
The lumberjack's mark was blue: a blue not found in nature.
I imagined you now to loathe what you built, even to hate
the siding's fit. The trunk went four feet through. But is not
all construction deconstruction? That tree had nested fowl.
It had harbored bugs in their millions. Each of its boughs
might have a tale to tell, had it a tongue. But it had none.
Nor did we, either one. All at once we went silent.

        We stayed that way for a long
moment. There is a weevil that preys entirely on pine.
There is also the prominent caterpillar, and at odd times
even the pear thripps, the sugar farmer's bane, may wander
far off its course in its search for maple sap. Worms and flies
vanish, come, and vanish, and yet that pine has kept its grip.
We too, so far. Often the wind arrives. What's it looking for?

It bullies whatever is in its way. It shoulders things aside, breaks branch and blade. It roots in pigweed, clover, joe-pye weed, grass. At last it'll scour everything here, all we love. Why clear woods for lumber, some ask.

Well, clearly, people must live somewhere. What about those who have nothing? Even they must live somewhere. If in a cardboard box in a vacant lot, if in a piano crate, then a tree in some forest paid. On that day wind wasn't bluffing, but acting the tyrant. Crazy. So it flew, let go, our bird. To think of vacancy seemed easy. (I thought too of a pun on *lot,* but chose not to speak it.) Once you told a joke in a canoe. Night, only a moon-peel showing through. The joke: old. Yet an image lingers, priceless, beyond words: a boat vibrates in darkness. Our laughter shook it. Our canoe was wooden too. Yet who'll give up that image?

Not I, I say. Not I, regardless. But I will, I must at last. Are my sweeter images thus untrue to nature? Spring: warblers. In every season: rough language of ravens, grating. Summer: our favorite, cedar waxwing. There's the redpoll, the ruby-crowned kinglet, the junco, even sometimes the eagle, the swan. Always a crow. So on: the dove whose voice I may liken to a flute. A flute may be of metal. It may be wooden too. Need I speak further? Need I fall mute? And have you fallen out of this memory, Joe? You have not. You don't ever. In all that I say, there's a slap of your hammer coming through.

I anyhow believe I can hear it. And patience. Let it come too. Let the maudlin be countered, but also obliteration. I fear it. I don't sing the balm of nature. In mind I watch you wield the clapboard, hear your whisper, note a bird's withheld gesture and a doomed pine's shudder. My wind, like all words: chiefly a figure. We've seen beaver, and now and then otter. In a boat, we once doubled over with laughter, a moon casting its vague powder on the water. It is these that the wind seems after, these things I treasure. Yet until the time we go under, I'll think of us as brothers. How much more we'll see. And further—

we will have seen it together.

R.N., Women's Ward

One raves, manic, about her nightmares: tonight, it's bone-white stairs,
              Down which she fears . . .
One is begging for her mother's telephone number. She's seventy or older;
              Thus, the mother . . .
One won't leave her IV alone — she screams to the nurse that they're doing
                        her in.
              Now they've begun . . .
One requests that the shade be lifted, polite; and the R.N. consents, quiet,
              Even though outside . . .

Wanderer planets tilt in the early hours among the cold-bleached stars.
              Mad drunks in cars . . .
Is that a cardiac monitor beeping? No, it's the nurse's own soles, squeaking.
              One's vaguely pleading . . .
One betrays her pledge: No More Tobacco. One, considered cuckoo,
              Cries that she ought to . . .
On earth, hushed below, the nurse sees a pallid patina of snow,
              But showing through . . .

              One drops the puzzle onto the covers and mutters,
              What a single vertical word would do . . .
              he imagines connections from it to all the others.

One sleeps, depressed; one's restive, nattering; one needs a new dressing;
              Yet more demanding . . .
How to name the demanding thing? One's buzzer resonates again
              for the tired R.N.,
Who as a child once gazed from her own high room: clouds thronged the
                        milky moon,
              Then seemed to run . . .
And on the village pond, blanched in winter, sometimes a midnight skater,
              a silent figure . . .

Each voice is brittle, whether soft or hard; each demands to be heard.
What *was* the word . . . ?
Car, star, ice, manic, depressive, cloud, sole, planet:
She yet may find it . . .
Tube, stairs, cuckoo, monitor, smoke, snow, drunk, mother:
Again, the buzzer . . .
One is pale and needs to be transfused. It's time for the nurse to conclude.
Something shows through . . .

Athlete's Scars

The one on his left-hand thumb is so very old —
      from before clocks or graves — he forgets its occasion.
      Some boyish game, no doubt.
          For years the mark seemed almost a smile,
    jaunty, horizontal young-moon sliver.
    It sits a bit upward
    of a knuckle that's lately begun to ache and fatten.
    Wound-trace much thinner than once, original pain
    having sunk long since toward the heart
        like tackles half remembered,
    like the later cuts of half-remembered lovers,
    and even of children, friends.
    The scar still bends, but downward now, a grimace,
    a sinister frown to reprimand,
    as coaches did, a person so doubtful, graceless.

Right index: a **V**, unsubtle as hour hand or dagger.
    It points at his palm as if to slice
    across the clumsy lifeline
        but halts at the blue-spidered base of the finger.
    He's still alive, still longs to be Newcomb or Ford,
    great men he adored
    for showing nothing, ever, but purpose and grace.
    He'd die to have thrown like that, while someone said
    (a scout, no doubt, on the sideline),
        "It's the *scar* that gives his pitches those breaks,"
    while girls and coaches marveled. That wasn't the case.
    A painful, blundering kid,
    he stabbed this finger-flesh with his very own pen,
    begging autographs while overhead
    the sky — what else? — was devoid of signature, sign.

Till death he's still and only what he was.
　　　Much turns to pallor, nondescript, faint.
　　　Yet crises, vague or keen,
　　　　　are no doubt etched under all these scars.
　　　He feels for one of the keen: an opponent's stick,
　　　like a vaudeville hook,
　　　yanked at his neck, and down to the ice he went.
　　　He fell onto somebody's blade. Of course.
　　　Over his heart, the pain.
　　　　　He recalls the coach's odd satisfied look
at blood on his breast; how the wheels of the gurney squawked;
the stitches he got; and a nurse—
"so graceful," he mumbled, puffing the chloroform mask
with his longing, more than ever obtuse—
and her yawn as she studied the watch on her blemishless wrist.

2

From *Searching the Drowned Man*

(1980)

Searching the Drowned Man:
The Third Day

I don't like the idea
of what we're going to find.
   —Bill White, search boss

After the two days of oiled calm
that morning the wind
blew up, ranging Grand Lake in lines
of foam.   Depending
on how you felt about the idea,
dread or hope
picked up as well. He'd be on the eastern
shore, where pines
bowed inland in November's gale from north-
northwest.   At last
we'd find him in the gut by Kolekill Island,
bobbing on cobby
beachstones, bright in autumn sun
as a different prospect.
But in that small canoe, incon-
sequential splash
of green like an afterthought on the blue-
near-black of the lake,
I called up other images:
                              the whited
eye of the broke-kneed
timber horse that drifted against
the dam in town
in August, minnows schooled in the putrid
cave of stomach.

The bloated belly-up suckers that clogged
the Wabass culvert
after the logging crew blew up
that beaver flowage.
The nauseating stink of the mill
when the breeze comes south.
How few, I thought, can swim! I was
the lone exception,
I who had joined the search in my young
man's search of ideas.
My father, an uncle and aunt, a boyhood
friend had died
behind some curtains.
                              A raft of hooded
mergansers fell in
downwind of our ragged hunting flotilla,
the slightest of lees.
A fish hawk screamed just once above
and shot the blow
out of sight over Farm Cove Mountain, whose bald
top winnowed clouds
like chaff as they galloped past. My knuckles
ached on the paddle.
I strained to store these signals up.
One day they'd be
the recollected lineaments
of what I'd found,
what felt.   And what
could I have been expecting, the Angel
Death? On finding
the man, the canoes to eddy like leaves
and blow off the map?
                              Did I hunt some grim articulation
from grinning lips
of the victim (who after all was only
the half-wit Lowery
from Springfield whom I half knew, who never
had any luck)?

Whatever I'd thought,
it wasn't this
declarativeness, a face that looked
engaged by plainest ideas: Now where
did I leave my jacket,
shoes? Hands raised up as if
to ward off gnats.
The body whole in its nondescript suit
of fishing clothes.
Flesh unrent by imagined turtles
who sink into boredom
as winter peeks through the fall, though clouds
and lake and mountain
and wind go on
as they have gone without repose.

Young Man Leaving Home

Over the dropped eggs and hash, his elders
poured unaccustomed benedictions.

The morning broke fair, but they
insisted on sensing rain.

That last spring, after so many,
the tree with the rope swing blossomed,

random plum blooms dropping groundward
where the playhouse leaned.

Later, the tracks with their switchbacks among
the shanties outside the station

had a somewhat surprising Protestant look
of a hopeless proposition.

Adieu: to the father who fobbed and fondled
his watch, at the end of his chain,

whose simple grief no halting final
declaration seemed to soften;

to the mother feigning impatience
with the lateness of the train.

They. Tree. House. Yard.
All had called for his valediction,

but now was already the hour prior
to greeting whatever it is that this is,

hour of assembly, of public instead
of certain longed-for private kisses,

hour of livered grandmothers, aunts,
whose cheeks the plain tears stained . . .

It passed in the fashion of dreams, at once
chaotic and sluggish.

En route: in silence, he hailed The Future,
that unimaginable lode of riches,

this hero, composed of a dozen young rebels
out of thin novels, groaning with luggage.

To the Summer Sweethearts

The easiness of August night:
a fall of meteors,
moths jewel my house

across the lane, I float
in the fire-pond, in the light-
riffled fire-pond. Cattails puff
their buoyant seed. The tadpoles
have absorbed their tails:
they hum and pause and hum.

Innocent, I ask you in.

The egg-rich mayflies dip and rise,
dimple the surface, die.
The silver guppies sip them.

Come sit, at least, composite
(eyes of Margot, Susie's hair,
the even smile of Sarah),
there on the bank.
You've seen the evil-looking turtles,
but sweetheart they never bite.

There. There.
Let's have a look at you.

Listen to the whippoorwill
chuck-will's-widow,
nightjar.

Night Message for Ted in the South

Neat as a knife, last night's storm tore
in two the tree that marks this trail.
That moony glim in the trunk's dust core
is foxfire, the light—they say—in hell.

Your ma wouldn't talk to your papa. He,
a preacher unfrocked for some philander,
raised prize white goats for the fairs, and she
raised roses. Somehow, the goats would wander

out of their pens to eat the flowers.
For which she shot them. You got a taste
for walks at dark. Clocks slouched the hours,
groaned arpeggios. Your parents paced

in separate rooms, black housemaids yawned
a final time, and heaved downhill to bed.
A hound, far off, would bawl the swamp;
the junebugs cracked against you, you said,

and in the pine-straw, rodents chittered.
Later, you joked at what neighbors called
"those folks on the hill." But an older sister
stayed there and died. The sheriff hauled

your broken brother, wild drunk, to prison.
Gone north, you hiked now in lead-filled air
among the pigeons. I'd come to listen
to the family farce, or else to hear

you dream out loud of your rambling nights.
At dark, we sat where bluesmen blew
their down-home runs under muted lights.
The shimmering horns reminded you,

you'd tell me, of the foxfire.
In the end, you moved back south, and I
went the other way: up here.
Still, in your letters, you would say

(before they stopped) how the very ground
you walked at sundown refused to alter,
how blooming in night-light you sometimes found
a rusted cartridge or a goat's rotted halter.

Here, a broken tree gaps pale.
Signs must tell us where we are,
or nothing. All the brooks are full
of the cleft moon cruising down the stars.

The President of Flowers

His wife referred to him as "Honey-Dripper,"
and it's true, in memory there is a sweet
association—sugared talk and whiff
of Sweet William, citric tang of the compost heap
in which his soft black hand threw everything,
even jars and bottles, for "glass ain't a thing
but sand blowed up, and sand it's bound to be
again one day." By which he must have meant,
though I was full of adolescent rage
and couldn't know it then, that death
was a thing too individual to count
for much among so many grander patterns.

                                              I only
sought to tell the old man truth: "Great God!
The black man in this land has no damned power!"
He warned me not to curse, then laughed like wind
along my parents' cherry orchard, nights:
"Son, I am the President of Flowers."
Poppies showed him, as they showed to no one else,
their bashful tongues. I swore that apples hung
in clusters before their blossoms fell away.
Exotic currants swelled our silver platter.
He grew a Pennsylvania avocado,
the only one I've ever seen, or heard of.
And then, toward fall, that strangest bloom—his cancer.

But he bent with it as he was used to bending,
and grapes came on more purple than before.
He gave up water, told me how the pain
would die of drought. He drove his truck to Georgia,
a visit to the family. There, he dug

a payload full of Dixie loam because
our Iris bed was full of bugs with claws.
"That red will quick-walk those old rascals down."
And *something* made them go. His death was like him,
slow: in alien odors of his darkened
house I sensed him—temples falling in,
a boyish skin, hands kneading at the folds—
and inhaled the jab of ruined marigolds.

In memory of Alex Lewis

For My Father, Who Hunted

. . . great as is the pleasure of becoming
acquainted with the stars and planets,
greater still the joy of recognizing them
as friends, returning after absence . . .
 —A Beginner's Star Book

A late beginner, I was struggling with
an early chapter: "Learning to Observe."
I have no faith in stars, in omens—nothing
there prepared me for the uncle's phone call

or the nothings sent back from the hospital,
laid out: a watch, a dollar nine in coin;
yet I hold, despite disastrous evidence,
a faith in language: *planet*, say,

from dim old names for *wanderer*. It has no place
that's certain like the stars'. Come near,
it kindles in the sky; or, wandered off,
it loses glory: that I've learned

is "occultation." Now all detail shines,
with a trace of brightness recognized,
though words obscure: the pheasant's fire
of feather in the dark of afternoon;

river waves rebounding noon's white slap;
the pickerelweed at false dawn flickered orange
above my spread of decoys.   All
have, in your absence, influence; and down,

as if to swing a leg across our log fence,
climbs Orion.   Or minutiae
rise up in mind and air: your wallet
spilling silver and your watch

in constellation, sweep hand sweeping back
the seconds, minutes fallen down.

Night Patrol: The Ancestral House

For A. B. Paulson

As he shakes it out,
his uncle's pup tent
exhales a cloud of moths, his army
outfit—at ease in a corner—
glows in a slick of camphor.

His generations sleep.
He steals
to each extreme: top floor and basement
and storage closet, clothes hung there like thieves.
Brocade on the shelves

handed from daughter
to daughter to daughter;
in a wicker case, a wedding photo
of elders unknown: the man's look is hard;
in the background a bugler, a color guard.

The return is a silence
broken only
by the lurch of a water pump, unsteady
as parents' snoring, the boiler's hum.
A small boy's drum

detects his parade
on the stairs—its springs
shift and whisper like weeds. The costumes . . .
some power that he would put on.
Here, a prayer book bound in silver
pulses in darkness like a clot of phosphor.

There, the navy
airplane he never
finished assembling, that Christmas dawn,
because of some battle with his dead father
that his dead mother thought was beneath her.

His generations
breathe at the ends
of old corridors. At attention,
he stands;
the regimented hours shrink
close, close around him, then break rank.

The Train Out

Fluff from his lap robe hangs in a rift
in the curtains, as his eyes ungum.
Nebraska yawns. Mergansers shift
in their mudholes. Morning: aluminum
track sheds begin to flare.

Blood ticks in his temples. Where
did he toss his coat, his keys?
As well in Topeka. Inanities
from a dream of her linger—a china jug,
hot liquor, a room

he cannot place. A tinsel bug
revives against the kindling panes.
Stiff old porters in the corridor
swear to a time when "a train was a train,"
mutter against the diesel's roar.

A green dead dawn . . .
All borders are ends . . .
He conjures a cove; a bed; a song;
rings and a necklace; a barbered lawn.

A catalog past. Old words, thick as wax.
Exhaust expires in a feint of wind,
and the sun glows dull on the tracks.

Night Trip across the Chesapeake and After

Mind a clutter: sick with love for another
woman, and set on murder (wildfowl would dive
next day to our brush-built blind). The diesel smeared
air with its fumes. Its wake roiled clumps of phosphor.
The hunters' "paradise" was a spit of land to the north
of Tangier Island. Dragged up from a barge, tin trailers
shuddered to windward amid knife-thin headstones
with jackets of slime. The marsh to the south was rank
with ages of feather-strewn nests and tangled lines
for crab, fish, otter. It weltered in weather,
sighing resignation.   The cooking station
reeked coal oil and antimacassars drenched
in sweat and the cheap pomade of insular men
and women. One saw one's life. A clotted flock
of newsy letters, cozy ancestral bones
that leaned from too many mantelpieces, squalid
crowd to be joined, babies' playthings, spattered
food, old grease in a covey of rusted spiders.

Come dawn, they swarmed: inedible shags and scoters.
They croaked black warning against desire.
Barnacles crept observably over the wharf posts,
thickened with ruin. The rain was steady, soaking.
Thoughts were kin to the wrack of lowest tide.
The mudflats smelled, O God, like hell.   The front
came suddenly on, from an antithetical quarter:
a cobalt-colored sky advanced against
the obvious wind. The boats of oyster dredgers
weighed their anchors, scudding free as stallions.
"Don't know what's in that rim," said Don our guide,
a different hue in his eyes. Rafts of coots

and trash ducks rose, headed for weedy bayou,
moss-choked brake.   Only the trumpeting hosts
of swans flew pure and wonderful into the weather.
Don the guide spat his cud of Red Man away,
declaring, "I'd just as soon shoot down an angel."
A cold breath swept the bay.

For My Son Creston at the Solstice

I've made a life.   Walking these ridges at dawn,
even in winter, when it seems no dawn will come:
pitiable minutes of daylight front the dark,
the wild things' tracks become so frozen-rimmed
my dogs ignore them.   Late into morning, owls
still whiffle past.   I tell myself that we
are December children, Creston.   We ought to know
births, beginnings out of the least suggestion.
In your high-built bed you're dreaming now, I'll guess,
of comic book heroes facing almighty space.
They never fail.   The snow's untimely deep,
so I follow my own old trail: to ramble off
today would be to fall to the throbbing knees,
reminders of old injury, the treacherous
crust would chip at my blood.   Walking these ridges,
I tell myself I've made a kind of life.

Now sleep.   In time you'll learn the signs I have
by heart.   A small bird's track.   See how he steps
and stops and pecks.   You'll notice how one toe
is missing at the knuckle, his print a compass rose
without an East.   Here he flutters (wingtips
brushing the dust), lands and cocks his head.
I'd almost said this silly ball of fluff
and I were of one mind. True, if at all,
by half or less. His mind is not on love.
He sensed that there was danger from on high
(that's why he skipped), but didn't wonder what
it was. An ice storm's beaten down the hemlock
here. I see the house. The fluming chimneys,
snow dams on the eaves. Breathing hard, I whisper,

"I've made a life," dream your mother risen,
your sister gazing at the mystery of her toes,

your morning clear before you as a pasture
after blizzard. Circling west, I drop
down to last August's campsite, where we cooked
and sang. So help me God, you'll never know
how long—while summer's light kept hovering over
Stonehouse Mountain—I sat before the tent flap,
far more crazy than I'd ever been, a sentry
warding off vague phantoms.   The slow-winged dark
filled with boding nightbirds, more single-minded
than I was or am. You were uncanny white
as snow. The canvas caught up the pathetic
sweetness of your breath.   I wept, the way a phony
hero does, exposed.   By now you're clothed.
Look.   The hares have shambled through our fireplace
on their run.   I'll tear away the hardpack.   There!
Old coals are flaring in the fierce new sun.

Band Concert

The bus, like a dozing monster,
nods yellow in high summer's grass
by the monument. We read its legend:
McCutcheon's Student Band.

All unchanged, they do the standards:
"Semper Fidelis," "A Grand Old Flag,"
assorted Sousas. The saxes crack
a note behind. McCutcheon beams.

The grocer dances to "Don't Fence Me In"
with a farmer's daughter. Two grim
Mormons stray among the pickup trucks,
dark volumes in their hands;

townsmen palm their beers and blush
their choked-down laughter.
Now the marching: vague hints of footwork.
And what if one day we do go under?

The kids whirl, frantic, on the seeding green.
The same plump blonde dips her baton
in kerosene. The finale flames
when she sparks her lighter.

The distant ocean blows thickly in-
to night that lies down soft on the crowd.
Moths and car horns swim the air.
July the Fourth, and more than ever

the old folks stiffen to "The Star-Spangled Banner."
Then everyone sings "Let the Rest of the World
Go By." And rapt, at the edge of things,
McCutcheon glows in a flick of thunder.

Drooge's Barn

Look if you like
through the roof beams;
but don't compare them to ribs.

Knock at the empty troughs.
You will not get a ghost's halloo
nor, failing, find your subject

in the silence. Stones in the cellar,
boards on the floor, are stones and boards,
not crying, not refusing to cry.

Yet of course you insist
on listening. And what you hear is a hound,
ragging the same white hare by moon

that he ragged all day by day.
His voice is a chop—like a hound's voice,
not an ax, a hoe, an adz.

Through the adz-smoothed beams
you find the familiar moon.
If it throws hieroglyphs on the walls,

it does so according to laws.
Underfoot, the chicken dust is hard
as slate, your breath is a vertical string

on nights like this so clear
you are aching to call them uncanny.
But the barn sags according to laws—

climate, time, and taxes.
Make no room for magic,
make no room for despair.

The dog's tune doubles and redoubles,
the punk in the floorboards glows, the moon
divides, beam after beam.

For Don C., against a Proverb

The simple are killed by their turning away.
   —Proverbs

I use examples:
you blew away

an insect's froth
to find him hidden

as in a pew.
I've seen you kneel

to sniff a stone
or chafe a bone,

bringing the full-fleshed,
fly-strafed, stamping

beast to mind.
Once, bent beachward

at the lake, you tried
to name the maker

of some human track,
imagine his mission,

his conversation.
Don, for you

I'm flouting Scripture.
Spiders sew

the woods together.
Limb to limb.

The sun assumes
one color, then

another, others.
Likewise moon

and dust and dew.
Your sermon was weather,

things, stars:
now *they* could write

their meanings, and none
was a dream of some

dim future. Home
for you was always

salt scent that rose
from working clothes,

the snap and hiss
in a stewpot, blood

and down on wife
and sons amid

the frantic dance
of slaughtered chickens,

agony
about the ribs

where love laid on
a velvet whip.

I've thought of the death,
of how some death

like yours should make
the Proverbs blanch

in shame. I bring
to mind the hand,

hard-horned and bursting
pods to see

familiar seeds
take wind. They rise

at dawn against
the whitening sky

like those last hardy
melancholy

stars afloat
in bright new morning—

stars that won't
put themselves out

nor quite turn out
till they are blown out.

Elegy at Peter Dana Point

For Creston MacArthur (1917–76)

Strips of shingle and bright can torn
from shack roofs, salt and sand, and saw-
dust from the housing project, fly in a wind
that drives the lake in a wild winter thaw.
A single high-top sneaker wheels
crazy on its lace, slipknotted to a limb.
Dogs hunker, cringe, and moan
against the north wall of a shed of tin,
where half untacked a poster peels
itself away: "Keep Maine's Forests Green."

The Indian point: the men in clean
white shirts, bought in town at the clean-out sale,
and mostly down on luck. Old Lola still gets on,
though his one good eye is pale
as powdered mustard. His oldest son,
the home-run hitter, rolls on the foot
shot up in Vietnam. They never did
find that ball he hit
in the Topsfield game, the one
the boys took in the bottom

of the ninth. What in Christ's gotten
into the weather? The power's failed
from here to the coast. No radio, no forecast.
And the oldest woman out here can't think
of such a day, so early. In bed
at home, she nurses the hurt in her black last
tooth: she fetches a drink

against it—hot liquor for her failed
old jaws and her hands, all gnarled and red
by the stove. The crack

of weather jitters her. All this wreck—
high water and wind and loss of power—
settles down on this hour.
She calls it a sign, and so do we,
less certain what we mean. Snowdrops hiss
against the windows. A churchyard tree is down,
branches snapped like savaged flowers.
What elegy in the face of this?
Perhaps we'll remember your own bold song,
to the music of an old-time sawyers' band:

"St. Regis thinks it owns the land
Where we hunt the ducks and geese;
St. Regis must be getting poor,
They want a dollar's lease.
We'll see they never get that fee,
For we've got things well in hand;
And St. Regis may be told someday
The MacArthurs own the land."
I remember one fall a single loon, calling for open water.

Today, another loon sculls in midwinter
on Long Lake. A raven pumps and swerves
overhead, fighting a blast of sky.
Workmen in khaki lift steel hats
as you roll by.
Fox tracks,
deer tracks
pick through the graves.
In the brush, the rusted head of an ax.
All your mourners know what they're weeping for

in the gaps of this mud-and-thunder roar;
but a few stand out, like beaver huts:
Lola and Leo, and old Earl, grim
as always, who called you "Gus";

and straight as a string your Uncle Jim,
with his strawberry nose, and full of rye;
"Three-Dollar" Bill, who blinks his eyes
like an owl; and down from Milltown, half-breed Dave,
the one you called "The Blue-Eyed Brave,"
who called you "Warden's Nightmare."

Something has changed in the air.
You almost smell spring, but not as it was,
now with the speedboats, the long-log saws,
electric fish-finders, and the company!
Sponging a buck to lie on the ground!
We'd have seen they never got that fee,
made sure they never found
the two of us, back far enough to scare them to death
in that corner near Thousand Acre Heath
with its early trout, where we saw the skulls

with antlers locked, in that slough so full
of trillium. Lovely, but how they reeked!
Like hell itself. Now Lola throws
a rose in the hole, and Earl a choke-
cherry sprig. Jim's drunken bunch blows
away, into cedar and oak.
And I, what posy do I have to leave?
A knot of grief,
the flowered turn of my eulogy:

"He loved life. He loved children. Good company.
Good times. From him, let us learn
that the sharing of pleasures is sacred to God."
(Yet I mean the smokes, rolled neat to burn
smooth and cool; that light on the ridge we never understood;
the first flight of woodcock; the last swarm of gnats;
the driftless calm on Flipper Creek,
when the geese eased by us, coasting the slick,
and we watched them, still as wildcats,
the near-purple sheen of their heads.)

The wind is suddenly dead,
its absence deep as was its rage.

The sun winds through the trees
and a white jay settles to gawk from the gate;
the minds of the mourners, of your age
or better, will rise
to Slewgundy, Pocumcus, Jones's Mistake
in the lull—for a moment, our small spites die.
The loon, alone, is fighting to fly
clear of its wake. We return

to our lives, away from The Burn,
from Bear Trap Landing, Jemison's Fate,
Unknown Stream, The Overnight Hole,
Dark Cove Mountain, Three Dawn Lake—
but old names blow through us like consecration.
Old names, old places, bring back you:
you knew them, touched them, boot, paddle, and pole.
Our elegy is your invention,
because you touched us, as seasons do.

3

From *The Floating Candles*

(1982)

Dirge for My Brother: Dawn to Dawn

Why, like a sentence that qualifies itself
to forestall the inevitable period, did I want your dying
protracted? Till the fourth dawn it was. Then wisps
of red cloud striped the sky, white
stars achieved their anabasis into blue.
I told you all your life to face the real.
And you have seen it, eyelids blasted full
and black with it. Preliminary calls
of birds, mere echoes of the great bombed bubble
of your mind. The complete works. The death so obvious, early.

1

Moonman! Another dawn. Always for you
a giant project. A stroke! Your awful explosion
mocks my cautious sermon: Recognize
Your Limits. You wouldn't till you had to. You,
hawk-high above the world. So little
comes, so little to listen for or see
in elegy. Only reverberant will
survives, and its blockaded ear, and eye.
I stare at the stars to envy their height. They're fading.
I hear pure bereavement rattle into the brain's
store: that region oddly military.
Moonman! Gung-ho commando! Your cycle shrieked
far out ahead of me. The gravel flew
like grapeshot out of a turn near Valley Forge.
You disappeared. I knew that barbed wire fence
was strewn with you before I geared down, twice,
and rounded the bend where—like the wonder of planets—
you floated the horizontal a skyscape away.

Later you stopped a while (I hadn't caught you).
Your wild eyes rocketed over my preachments of calm.

2

O say can you see some order, brother? Mine
has been another day's distracting syntax.
The birds resign with evening. The world doesn't give
a hoot or whistle. Love and hate convolve,
are hard to conquer. I still cannot resist
the inclinations of sentence. I cast mine wide
into darkness. Superior, till it drove you half past crazy.
Earlier still, like a sniper you trained a gun
on me, hid in a bush at dusk. You screeched
at my dovish pleadings: "Stay on neutral ground!"
I recall the manic orders, remember clear as sirens

the gun and bush: Browning, cardinal flower.
Within limits, my mind is clearer than ever. And yours?
For ninety-six hours a few poor straggling threads.
Artery, vein, blanched tatters of a flag,
of the mind that resisted internment. You flew at me quick,
drawing first blood with rock, shoe, stick. I waited
through the barrage, and generally so prevailed.
Yet Moonman! Your hand was open to others. A dog,
a child, the downcast. Always an easy touch.
I save some pictures of you, downtown. In one, your banner
fairly screams for THE END OF DISCRIMINATION
NOW! In another, you carry "Cherokee,"
that runaway on Chestnut Street, to drop her
at a preacher friend's: "Father, the girl's fourteen!"
Your mind can detect the rustle of city vultures
who'd swoop at her, but not—the preacher chuckles—
how her Jersey parents will wail when they discover
their vagabond nestling nesting with Reverend Nigger.
The big twin coughed, exploded, and you lit out
—like a hawk, an eagle, Buck Rogers, Batman, Superman—Moonman!

down to that club (The Gilded Cage) where bluesmen
whined, "Don't the Moon Look Pretty, Shining Down
Through the Trees?" Then off again, soaring the asphalt,
tailpipes flaring like moon itself. It grinned
from crater to crater. In triumph, pleasure? Here lies
no mighty chief or leader as the world will measure
such a thing, and yet I feel the republic
stumble, crack. The mourners—the humble, rich,
the white and black—all look away. And I
among them. I, whose words should blast like twenty-one cannons . . .

A Natural Shame

The moon's small aura pins
the shadow of the sleeping children's
hobbyhorse down, black comic
monster, flat to the floor.
And I, inept at prayer,
clutching the bedclothes, I picture
wreck, gun, epidemic.
Tabloid headlines figure
in the elm tree's leaves.   Unmoored,
a shingle flaps into air.
Snapped from sleep so short
it only dried the throat
by a phrase: "A natural shame . . ."
As if in her long career
nature had ever known shame—
this sentence, out of the country
junkyard that is the mind
untended, wakes me to sentry
duty. Unsettled by wind,
my old dog clicks along
the halls in disrepair.
Their ancestors' cells among
the bloodways of the babies
conspire, too soon, too soon.
The will would impose its stasis,
but in every pictured scene
I envision a moving thing:
bicycle tire spinning,

glucose bottle dripping
like heartbreak, murderer fleeing,
solid realist, earth, unfurling
into romantic flight,
ink going white.

Chanty: Cleaning the River-Driver

For Larry Lieberman

In the dry town he drank
vanilla extract, tiny
bottles turning the barky
gums a hue of inland
myrtle. I shaved him Sunday
mornings, he shook and stank
and cursed (even me sometimes).
I'd studied Billy Grimes,
who'd scouted the logjams,
back straight up on the seat
of the boat. Stiff whiskers
resisting wind. One day
I dreamed we'd take to the river,
the sea-run salmons' beat
where he'd been a driver, plunge
paddles, skirting the half-sunk
deadheads, the eddies that strained them
till they sang in spume and sun.
Billy got happy-drunk.
Plunging the brush,
I worked the soapsuds in
those years, until inside
his sweat-stained union suit
he shrank. I grew on, saving
a picture while jetsam of glass,
beard and soap swelled wide
around the wicker armchair,
and chaw plugs, crushed

to a texture of peat or soot,
sank in the knotty cedar
of his cabin floor. I side-
stepped, cautious, wielding
the razor, child's eyes searching
the curious maplike lines
of Billy Grimes's face.
A rite that led all Lord's Days
back to a source, or end.
"I don't throw no bouquets,
you know, but you're a friend,
boy. . . . Fetch me another."
As he warmed and steadied, lather
sank like froth in sand.
The riverman's arms were good
where they met the foam-white shoulder.
The big thighs tensed when he stood,
and happy words made waves
of tendon in his neck, and flowed
into his eyes. He'd holler
at last, "Goddam, let's go
right off downriver, son.
The ocean! The Hundred Islands!
A month on every one!"
Then he shambled out to the shade
where he dozed till after noon,
slumped against a tree,
though the wind—faint-scented with sea—
could cut you like a blade.

There Should Have Been

With evening the groom and bride in groundfog
should have mounted the flatbed wagon, drawn
into the orchard by a vast dappled bullock.
Deer—tall stag, keen doe—should have come

so lacily gliding you'd have trouble to tell
their shapes apart from the onrushing mist.
An uncle was seated beside me. He held
white folds of my shirt collar locked in a fist.

He rumbled: "My dancing days are all over,"
showing the blue stub under his knee
where skin like a windfall plum's was gathered.
I started. He gathered me back to see.

The buck's high rack would be velvet by rights,
would sparkle—I thought—with beads of the fog
in the firelight. Because there should have been firelight,
costume, concertina, song.

A wattled aunt secretly loosened a stay.
They could have been lovely, the bride and the groom,
waltzing together on pale tumbled blooms.
I thought how a falling star might display

the company's tears, good bubbles of wine,
the rings of emerald newts on the pond
in mating embrace. The close room was stained,
the hallways were humid, with beer and with rum.

The uncle insisted on hauling the needle
back to the same first groove, every dance.
He hummed a rough note under Ella Fitzgerald's
"Love for Sale." The party winced

at his crippled taste. Outside the rain
delivered howls from the turnpike, hammers,
drills, and curses of masons and carpenters
working all night on "Whispering Pines,

Half-Acre Estates" — they were "Coming Soon!" —
across the fields. My father started
the rust-pitted Chevy for home at one.
Leg propped on the seat, my uncle farted

and snored. My mother angled her nose
to the window. The asphalt wrinkled with steam.
There should have been some way of escape
for the lumpish opossum pair on the road,

dazed as the couple I'd saved from the cake,
jacked in their tracks by the onrushing beams.

To a Surgeon

For Richard Selzer

Nights, the stars
like polyps arrange
themselves in a body
I envision as world.
Or I say they hang
like clustered fates
waiting to fall
on the body, curses,
high pains that at last
will make us strange.

Your vision's straight
as razors, earned
each day gowned green,
your eye is schooled
and hands have learned
excision of trope.
Still in the theater,
I only seem
to unmask myself.
I borrow my terms

as I stretch this world
before you, body
and lumpish brain
and untrue dream
so often lashed
together by bloody
threads of figure,

like wildflowers sewn
in the stammering throat
of a brook, or muddy

lichens gathered
on the oaks' gnarled chests.
My children, exotic
and restless as cancer,
natter for breakfast.
Through frost-laced panes
I watch two hills
sag off the sun
and lust to be on them,
for the mind says *breasts*

though it knows that weather
has capped them with ice,
so slightly does world
conform to desire.
If hills are breasts,
how will we hide there
the winter-sick rabbits
thick as ward patients,
white, on the hillsides
waiting for death?

How account for the way
last autumn the flames
cauterized acres?
. . . The moon struggles up,
and the heart, that lame
redded hare, and woman
bloods to the moon.
The hills become beauty,
like health. A kestrel
rides the first beam

like the first pure thought
of the one who survived,
or a child who's swum
through amnios rank

as a new spring tide.
The metaphors clot
my conning of world's
immense operation,
and I'd lay myself open
for one hour, clarified,

malign or benign.
Sure eye, sure hand.
You shrug off my envy,
old sawbones plumbing
goiter and wen,
but you bend to the body
and worlds — moon, rabbit,
child, sun,
hawk, father,
high stars — attend.

Bernie's Quick-Shave (1968)

At dawn three shearsmen
dress in white, exact
non-shade of the blank
prospect that they'll encounter
but — out of their courage —
they refuse to acknowledge.
Or is it their impotence?
Out on the Green,
which in this February
is more in fact
a White, long-haired
students from the college
return to their monuments of ice:
the carnival theme
this winter is *Life*
in the Future. Machines
in this fantastic tableau
are conceived to replace
all dulling labor.
The students in arrogance
consider *themselves* the Future.
Sad, the way
that Frank, Ed, Mike
— pale monoliths,
three plinths
behind the pane — all day
will regard these children in beards
and tattered pants
as the Future, too:
a season gone away
before its own arrival.

The chair keeps yawning like
a dead man's abandoned
recliner. The lather won't rise
to match the drifts
and windrows by their trailers.
It remains the latent billow
within their minds,
as fog and whitecap waves
become mere thought in sailors
grounded—vague things
to fill the void they prophesy
as yet another night
falls on the village
shops, forlorn and white
as those few unconsoling early stars.

At length, berobed,
they struggle to their cars,
whose windshields seem at first
to cloud with steam.
Their radios often bear them
news of former
clients now, last regulars
turned in this decade hairless
or thinly crowned with slow-
grown locks that shiver
in the frigid estate to which
their whiteness is witness . . .
The radios announce
old shavers gone,
like figures one has met
within a dream
or landscapes that will never
be replenished.
Snow drifts down like talcum.
But tomorrow dawn
they'll stand again,
tragic as winter gravestones,
those for whom some central thing has vanished.

Accident

In memory of Howard Moss

Never to remember
New York City
Mingus's splendid tirades
Chico Max
The MJQ or early Gerry
He rides
His bike shooting out of woods like a switchblade
Onto the lane
In our meadow where night air
Leaves a slick on the gravel. This dawn
Has no steam breathing through pavement cobbles
But a purple moth struggles
With the wet burden like Elvin
Jones in a gin-soaked club
And with his half-shucked shell
Into such brief improvisation
Of beauty that if the boy were nearer
Or it were an hour later
(Daytime frogs on the beat
Like morning cops—Ninth at Broadway, dawn,
Twenty years gone—
Or my daughter doing her scat
Voices drowning
The riff of wings like tiny high-hat cymbals)
I would never have noticed

The muted sun like Miles cuts through
The mist flumes' chorus
On the river where mayflies
Lose their shifting hold on pebbles
At the bottom and make their way up
And trout at their stations hover like trebles
In the hay-sweet hills
The I I think I am
Beats against the snare of the past
And sleep and dream
Hard case
My son repeats
The terrible solo again
And again in his seventh summer
That decrescendo
Dreaming his bike a flyer
Set for the moon like Diz
Last night my baby daughter
Poked a thumb at the ofay moon
And sang, "I want it." She thinks
It's Big Rock Candy. Meat fat and drink
Clash in my sour intestines
Like Monk's odd clusters in the old Half Note
The moth flies up
And clings in splendor to a screen

Hanging in country air
There's the boy's high wail
As his fender shivers like a tambourine

Battle

To the satisfied lookers-on

After George Bellows's "Both Members of This Club"

A lie of course, a lie accommodating
the time's loose law. Each fighter was
elected for the night—night of The Battle—
hurrahed or hissed, and then sent packing.
In the bottom quarter of the canvas, actual
members' faces, in death's-head grins and leers.
The colored boxer's face can't be distinguished
from the upper quarter's background of solid black.
The white boy wears a bloody makeup beard,
but it isn't makeup, is it? Their wrists seem soldered,
and the members' merry eyes suggest some joke,
as if a brass band's oompah beat were pulsing
and in parodic outrage both the boxers,
done with trading punches, had started waltzing.
But see the high-volt tension in the ropes,
the knees that flex so tight you'd think the caps
would burst the skin, and pectoral muscles show
the evening's fierceness.   So does the sad
contemplative look of a cornerman who grasps
some turn in the bout he doesn't like the look of.
We look, but can't determine what it is.
We say of the two, They are above it—gods.
We say, The ignorant lookers-on will sizzle
in hell, and that the painter knew it all.
Or that these Battlers both are made of oil

and water on a canvas—fabrications
accommodating a set of aesthetic laws.
Yet somewhere now an actual toilet bowl
stands ready to take the kidneys' ring of blood,
real blood, for somewhere there's a canvas
flecked with the actual colors of election.
This isn't that rose gore of old Romance.
The loser's eyes turn inward to the blackness.
The winner's eyes turn upward to the blackness.
We look, and say, The Battle is a dance.

The Floating Candles

For my brother Mahlon (1944-80)

You lit a firebrand:
old pine was best.
It lasted, the black
pitch fume cast odors
that, kindling a campfire
or such, today
can bring tears. You held
the torch to one dwarf
candle stub then another
and others till each
greased cup filled up
and the stiff wicks stood.
Ten minutes a candle,
but we were young
and minutes seemed long
as the whole vacation.
We chafed and quarreled.
The colors bled
like hues in jewels.
At last we carried
a tub of the things
down the path to the Swamp
Creek pond through seed-
heavy meadows where katydids
whined like wires
in mid-August air's
dense atmosphere.
An hour before bedtime.

Reluctant grownups
would trail behind,
bearing downhill
the same dull patter
and cups brimful
of rye, which they balanced
with the same rapt care
that balanced our load.
The bullfrogs twanged
till you touched a wick
with the stick, still flaming,
then quieted. We heard them
plop in the shallows,
deferring to fire,
and heard in the muck
turtles coasting in flight.
The night brought on
a small breeze to clear
the day that all day
had oppressed us, to dry
the sweat that our purposeful
hour had made,
to spread the glims
like dreamboats of glory
in invisible current.
That slow tug drew
the glowing flotilla
south to the dam.
The bank brush—hung
with gemmy bugs—shone
and made great shadows
as the candles slipped by,
erasing the banal
fat stars from the surface.
This was, you could say,
an early glimpse
of a later aesthetic.
Nonsense. We know
it was cruder than that

and profounder, far.
It showed us the way
the splendid can flare
despite the flow
of the common. Now,
despite the persistence
of heat and quarrel,
the thickness of wives
and children and time,
such shinings on water
are fact. Or sublime.

The Feud

I don't know your stories. This one here
is the meanest one I've got or ever hope to.
Less than a year ago. Last of November,
but hot by God! I saw the Walker gang,

lugging a little buck. (A sandwich size.
It *would* be. That bunch doesn't have the patience.
I'd passed up two no smaller, and in the end
the family had no venison that fall.)

I waved to them from the porch—they just looked up—
and turned away. I try to keep good terms
with everyone, but with a crowd like that
I don't do any more than necessary.

It wasn't too much cooler back inside.
A note from my wife on the table said the heat
had driven her and the kids to the town pond beach
to sit. That made some sense. It's the last that will.

I peeked out quick through the window as the Walkers'
truck ripped past, and said out loud, "Damn fools!"
The old man, Sanitary Jim they call him,
at the wheel, the rifles piled between

him and Step-and-a-Half, the crippled son.
In back, all smiles and sucking down his beer,
Short Jim and the deer. Now Short Jim seems all right.
To see his eyes, in fact, you'd call him shy.

He doesn't talk quite plain. Each word sounds like
a noise you'd hear from under shallow water.
I didn't give it too much thought till later,
when the wife and kids came home, and wanted to know

what in Jesus' name that awful smell was,
over the road? Turns out that Walker crew
had left their deer guts cooking in the sun.
And wasn't that just like them? Swear to God,

to leave that mess beside a neighbor's house
for stink, and for his dogs to gobble up?
And there was one thing more that puzzled me:
why wouldn't they take home that pile of guts

to feed *their* dogs? A worthless bunch—
the dogs, I mean, as well as them. You'd think
they wouldn't be above it. Every decent
dog they ever had was bullshit luck,

since every one they run is one they stole
or mooched out of the pound. You'll see them all,
hitched to one lone post, dung to the elbows,
and every time they get themselves a new one,

he'll have to fight it out until the others
either chew him up or give him up.
I guessed I'd do this feeding for them, so
I raked up all the lights into a bag

and after nightfall strewed them in their dooryard
with a note: "Since I'm not eating any deer meat,
I'd just as quick your guts rot somewhere else
as by my house." And signed my actual name.

The whole thing's clear as Judgment in my mind:
the sky was orange, the air so thick it burned
a man out of his senses. I'm the one.
And evening never seemed to cool me off,

though I'm a man whose aim is not to truck
in such a thing. I've lost most of my churching,
but don't believe in taking up with feuds.
I usually let the Good Lord have His vengeance.

Nothing any good has ever grown
out of revenge. So I was told in school

when I slapped up Lemmie Watson, because he broke
the little mill I built down on the brook.

And so I learned. I spent the afternoons
that week indoors, and I've been different since,
till this one day. Then something else took over.
There passed a week: they stove my mailbox up.

At least I don't know who in hell beside them
would have done it. I had a spare. (The Lord
knows why.) I cut a post and put it up,
and could have left the blessed fracas there,

and would have, as my wife advised me to.
And I agreed. I told myself all night,
my eyes wide open, lying there and chewing,
"Let it go." And would have, as I claim,

but two days passed, and they came hunting coons
on this side of the ridge. I heard their hounds.
(God knows what *they* were running. Hedgehogs? Skunks?
It could have been.) Out on the porch

I heard *tick-tick*. Dog paws, and all *my* dogs
began to yap and whine. I made a light.
Shaky, thin as Satan, a docktail bitch,
a black-and-tan (almost), was looking in.

I made of her. She followed me as if
I'd owned her all my life out to the kennel.
I stuck her in the empty run that was
Old Joe's before I had to put him down.

I filled a dish with meal. She was a wolf!
The first square feed she'd had in quite a time.
My wife kept asking what I could be up to.
Likes to worry. Next day I drove clear

to Axtonbury, to the county pound.
"This dog's been hanging round my house all week.
Don't know who she belongs to." Lies, of course.
I had her collar locked in the Chevy's glovebox.

I wouldn't harm a dog unless I had to,
and figured this one stood a better show
to make out at the pound than at the Walkers'.
But the Walkers didn't know that. Driving home,

I flung the collar in their dooryard. After dark,
and spitting snow, six inches by next day,
late in December now, toward Christmastime.
Things shifted into higher gear despite me.

Or on account of me. Why not be honest?
I know that nowadays it's not the fashion
to think a person's born what he becomes;
but Sanitary Jim, his wife and family:

I never gave it too much thought but must
have figured right along that they belonged
to that great crowd of folks who *don't* belong.
Their children wear their marks right on them: speech

you hardly understand, a rock and sway
where a normal boy would take an easy stride.
And in and out of jail. If they can't find
another bunch to fight with, why, they'll fight

with one another. (Sleep with one another
too, if talk can be believed. There are
two homely sisters in the mix as well.)
Short Jim beat an uncle or a cousin

—I disremember—beat him right to death.
(It's not the fashion either nowadays
to keep a violent man in jail. A month, no more,
goes by, and Short Jim's on the town again.)

But back to what I just began. The Walkers
are as bad as banty roosters, and I figured
they were meant somehow to be. Where most of us
are meant to eat one little peck of dirt,

they eat a truckload. Is it any wonder,
then, I didn't make a special point

of mixing with them? No more than I would
with any crowd that filthed itself that way.

But mix with them I did. It seemed as if
their style of working things reached up and grabbed me.
I was in the game so quick it turned my head.
The snow came on, the first big storm of winter,

that night I pulled the trick with the docktail's collar.
In the morning, barely filled, I saw their tracks
around my kennel. But *my* runs both are solid
chain-link, and the doors are padlocked shut.

They mean a thing or two to me, those dogs.
I keep the keys right on me. No one else
—no family, no good friend—can spring a dog
of mine. That way, I know they're there, or *with* me.

I'm only puzzled that they never growled. They do
as a rule. I was surely glad the Walkers hadn't
had the sense to bring along some poison.
A dog's a dog, which means he's five-eighths stomach.

Thinking on this gave me bad ideas.
But I'll get to that when time is right. For now,
I called myself a lucky fool, out loud,
and bolted both dogs shut inside their houses

nights. I judged this thing would soon blow over.
I burned a yardlight too, which I'd never done.
And that (I guessed) was the last they'd come past dark.
You know, the funny part of this whole battle

up to now, when you consider who
I'd got myself involved with, was that neither
side had come right out into the open.
The only thing I knew for sure they'd done

was leave a mess of guts out on my lawn.
The only thing for sure they knew of me—
that I returned that mess to its right home.
The mailbox and the collar and the tracks . . .

For all we either knew, the Boss was making
visions in our eyes which, feeling righteous,
we took upon our *selves* to figure out.
And since, between the parties, I guessed *I*

had better claim to righteousness than they did,
I'm the one who—thinking back—began
to read the signs according to my will.
How many times have village hoodlums stove

a mailbox up? Or just plain village kids?
How many times, to mention what comes next,
has one old drunk shitkicker or another
raised some hell outside Ray Lawson's Auction

and Commission Sales on Friday night? And still,
I judged it was the Walkers who had slashed
all four of my new pickup's summer tires.
(Four months had passed.) And judged it quick as God.

The pickup spraddled like a hog on ice. It cost me
two hundred dollars just to run it home.
Next day I passed Short Jim as he came out
of Brandon's store and sized him up, and looked

at him: a man who'd killed another man,
but shyness in his eyes. He looked away.
And if *I'd* looked away just then . . . Instead,
I saw a basket full of winter apples,

Baldwins mostly, full of slush and holes.
No wonder Brandon had that crop on sale!
Four cents each was asking more than enough
for winter apples still unsold in April.

If the top one hadn't had a hole as big,
almost, as half a dollar . . . By God, where
would we be now? But there it was, the hole,
and I got notions. Maybe fate is notions

that you might have left alone, but took instead.
I did. I bought that apple, and another

just for show. And a box of pellets, too—
more rat pellets than I ever needed,

more than I could stuff into that hole
and still have stay enough in the rotten skin
to hold them in enough to fool a hog
that he *had* an apple. Walkers' hog, I mean.

They penned her on the far side of the road
from where that firetrap shack of theirs was built.
I didn't set right out. That apple sat
as much as seven days up on a post

of metal in the shed, where even rats
—Lord! let alone my kids—could never reach it.
And it sat inside my mind. Especially nights.
Or say it burned, the while I cooled myself

—or tried to do, with every nerve and muscle—
in bed, and said the same thing over and over:
"Nothing good will ever grow from feuds."
And just to get the apple *out* of mind,

spoke such damn foolishness you never heard:
"Old Mother Hubbard," "Stars and Stripes Forever"
(tried to get the words of one to go
along with the rhymes and rhythms of the other).

Then went down that seventh night, as if it was
another person who was going down
inside the shed (because the person I
believed I was kept up the sermon: "Nothing

any good from any feud," and so on),
picked the apple down, and put it in
my pocket, and—the moon was full—began
the uphill climb across the ridge. To Walkers'.

Stopped for breath at height of land, I turned
to see the house, where everyone was sleeping,
wondered what they dreamed, and if their dreams
were wild as mine become when moon's like that—

they say there's nothing in it, but as God
will witness me, a full moon fills my head,
asleep or not, with every bad idea.
One spring, the moon that big, a skunk came calling

in the shed, and my fool tomcat gave a rush.
The smell was worse than death. It woke me up,
if I was sleeping (I'd been trying to),
and till the dawn arrived, for hours I felt

the stink was like a judgment: every sin
from when I was a child till then flew back
and played itself again before my eyes.
High on the ridge, I felt I might reach out

and touch that moon, it was so close, but felt
that if I reached it, somehow it would burn.
It was a copper color, almost orange,
like a fire that's just beginning to take hold.

Your mind plays tricks. You live a certain while
and all the spooky stories that you read
or hear become a part of memory,
and you can't help it, grown or not, sometimes

the damnedest foolishness can haunt you. Owls,
for instance. I know owls. How many nights
do they take up outside, and I don't think
a thing about it? *That* night, though,

a pair began close by me. I'd have run,
the Devil take me, if the light had been
just one shade brighter, I'd have run right home
to get out of the woods or else to guard

the house, the wife, the kids. I don't know which.
A rat or mouse would shuffle in the leaves
and I would circle twenty yards around it.
I was close to lost until I found the brook

and waded it on down. It was half past two.
The moon kept working higher till I saw

the hog shed just across the road from Walkers' house.
There wasn't that much difference in the two.

I'm a man can't stand a mess. But they,
the boys and Sanitary Jim. . . . Well, they
can stand it. Seems that that's the way
that they *prefer* it. That hovel for the pig

was made of cardboard, chimney pipe, and wanes.
They'd driven I don't know how many sections
of ladder, side by side, into the mud
for fencing. Come the thaw each year, the ground

will heave that ladder up, and then you'll find
a pig in someone's parsnips. Anyway,
I looked the matter over, and the worry
that I'd felt about the thing that I was doing—

well, it went away. I felt as pure
as any saint or choirboy hunkered there.
I crept up on my knees and clapped the gate
(a box spring from a kid's bed) so the pig

would have a peek. I don't know why, exactly,
but I felt like watching as she took the apple
from my hand. It wouldn't do to leave it.
She just inhaled it, didn't even chew.

I backed up to the brook and watched some more,
then stepped in quick, because that poison sow
began to blow and hoot just like a bear.
The job was done. I hadn't left a track.

I don't know just what you'll make of this:
I fairly marched back up across the ridge
as if I made that climb four times a day.
The air was cold and sweet and clear, the way

it is when you can see the moon so plain.
I walked on to a beat and sang the hymns
—or sang them to myself—I'd got by heart
so many years before: "Old Rugged Cross"

and "Onward Christian Soldiers" and "Amazing
Grace," and never noticed how the cold
had numbed my feet till I was back in bed.
No one woke up. I slept two righteous hours.

You jump into a feud, and every trick's
like one more piece of kindling on the fire.
That's how I think of it, and you'll see why.
Come evening of the next day, I was sick.

You don't go paddling nighttimes in a brook
in April, and expect it's just a trick.
All night it felt like someone had a flatiron
and kept laying it between my shoulder blades.

My feet and legs were colored like old ashes.
My throat was sore enough I couldn't speak.
My wife, who didn't have a small idea
of where I'd been beside beneath the quilts,

lay it all to how I carried on.
"You've heard the old expression, 'sick with worry.'
That's what you've brought yourself, I think, from scheming
on those godforsaken Walkers." She was right,

but not the way she thought she was. In time,
there wasn't any use, I had to go
down to the clinic, twenty miles away.
You know those places: wait there half a day,

then let them pound you, scratch their heads, and scratch
some foolishness on a scrap of paper, wait
the other half while the druggist dubs around
to find the thing he's after. Come home poor.

If it was only poor that I came home!
I drove through town at fifteen miles an hour.
Swear to God I couldn't wheel it faster,
the way I was. It was a job to push

the throttle down, and I could scarcely see,
so blinked my eyes a time or two when I reached

the flat out by the pond. Above the ridge
the sky was copper orange, and thick black smoke

was flying up to heaven, straight as string.
I thought I felt the heat. (But that was fever.)
By Jesus, that was *my* house. "Chimney fire,"
I said out loud, or loud as I could talk,

my throat ached so. The words were just a whisper,
and they sounded wrong the minute they came out.
I felt like I would die from all this sickness.
They called me "walking wounded" at the clinic:

pneumonia, but just barely, in one lung;
but now I felt my blood would burst the skin
and I'd just up and die inside that truck.
I squinched my eyes and lay the throttle on.

I meant to do some good before I died.
My wife was wrestling with a metal ladder
that had sat outside all winter, though I'd meant
to get it under cover every day.

I used it cleaning chimneys. It was stuck
in puddle ice beside the western wall
I jumped out of the truck before it stopped,
and fell, and got back up, sweet Christ,

I tried to run, and every step I took
was like a step you take in dreams, the space
from road to house seemed fifteen thousand miles.
I stumbled to the shed and grabbed an ax

and put it to the ground to free the ladder,
but the ground just wouldn't give the damned thing up,
and every lick was like I swung the ax
from under water. I had no more force

than a kid or cripple. My kid, meanwhile, cried
from behind a big storm window, "Daddy? Daddy?"
It sounded like a question. I gave up
and tried to call back up to him. I couldn't.

My words were nothing more than little squeaks,
and when they did come out, they were not plain.
And so my wife began to call the boy,
"Throw something through the window and jump out!"

He threw a model boat, a book, a drumstick.
He couldn't make a crack. I flung the ax.
It missed by half a mile. I threw again
and broke a hole, and scared the boy back in.

That was the last I saw him. Like a woman
sighing, that old house huffed once and fell.
Out back, beside the kennel, our baby daughter
danced and giggled to hear the howling dogs.

I went into dead faint. And hell could come
for all of me. And that is what has come.
Thirty years gone by since Lemmie Watson
broke my little mill of sticks and weeds

down by the brook, and I kicked the tar from him
and stayed indoors all week when school let out.
And Mrs. What's-Her-Name, I disremember,
fussing at her desk, would shake her head

and ask out loud if one small paddle wheel
was worth all this? I had to answer No.
I had to write it down, "No good can grow
from any feud." I wrote it fifty times

each afternoon. And then one afternoon
the Walker crew laid down a string of guts
across the road . . . The part of life you think
you've got done living lies in wait like Satan.

For me, it was revenge. And what to do
right now? The house is gone, the boy, and I
believe I know just how they came to be.
But do I? Do I know what led to what

or who's to blame? This time I'll let it go.
No man can find revenge for a thing like this.
They say revenge is something for the Lord.
And let Him have it. Him, such as He is.

4

From *No Sign*

(1987)

Fall

Carpenter, Mechanic, and I:
it is our yearly hunting trip
to this game-rich, splendid, dirt-poor margin
of Maine. There is always rain and a gale,
and one or two
bluebird days just to break the heart.
We're good at this thing we do,
but for each bird that falls,
three get by us and go
wherever the things that get by us go.

To the realm of baby shoe and milk tooth;
kingdom of traduced early vow,
of the hedge's ghost, humming with rabbit and rodent,
under the mall's macadam. All that seemed
fixed in the eye.   I,
according to Mechanic,
is too melancoholic. Yes, says Carpenter,
and talks when he ought to be doing.
We all watch the canny pointer, with her nose
like a Geiger counter.

"There's not much gets by *her*,"
we repeat each year, admiring, after she's flashed on point
and *shaaa!*—in redundant wind another grouse flies wild.
Air and ridge and water now all take
the color of week-old blood. Or years-old ink.
We are such friends it's sad.
Not long before we stalk before winter the heavy-horned
bucks that slide past,

spirit-quiet, in spare brush.
Then Carpenter and Mechanic in their loud mackinaws will seem

interruptions on the skyline of the sky's
clean slate. And so will I.

After Labor Day

Your son is seven years dead.
"But it seems," I said, seeing your face
buckle in mid-conversation
as over the fields came winging the trebles
of children at holiday play—
I said, "But it seems like yesterday."

"No," you said,
"Like today."

In the first of the black fall drizzles,
in a morning when world's-end seems to hover
too near, the early fallen
leaves slick on the highway as blood,
the yellow ball had spun to a halt
on the white line:
your small child scurried there like an ignorant vole . . .

It is the time of year
when hawks rush down the pass where you live,
but the heat last weekend held them
northward. So grounded, we talked like voluble schoolkids
inside, instead. —Or I did.
You lost in thought, dark brows arched
like the wings of birds at travel,
or soaring to hide, or seek.

At home, I recall your eagle visage, how now
and then it falls
just so. In the change, in the first cold autumn rain,
I play at identification.

I imagine how red-tail, Cooper's,
rough-leg, little blue darter,
and the odd outsider—Swainson's, say—
now pass you by,
as at home in my study I watch
two scruffy starlings on a wire outside
fronting what they seem to have
no choice but to front
till one peels off, is sucked it seems into woods, and through
the glass I yet can hear him.
His croaks come this way, as if the other
were the one who had vanished, not he.

Just so lost children imagine
their parents are lost, not they.
"Where did you go?" they chirp, as if we hadn't been
shrieking, searching.
Or as if our terror had been a game.

It's the season of the mushroom all of a sudden.

Closed though my window is,
over the vapors and trees I also hear
the doubled scream of a kestrel.

You heard, these seven years have heard, the swish
of tandem tires through puddles,
the last gasps
of airbrakes, screams.
And loud as unthinkable detonation
—or so at least in dreams it seems—
the impact:

every outside sound raced clear to you.
But walls and panes cut short your shouts
from inside the house,
as if *you* were the small boy
to whom the remote roar
of the world was suddenly apparent,
yet whose voice was as in dreams
unheard or worse: irrelevant.

In the lulls, by way of compensation,
I talked the holiday away.
Talked and talked and
talked and talked
and cataloged the game:
I called attention
to early goldeneyes out on the marsh;
to the way in later light
—like cheap raincoats—the feather's colors
on the backs of ducks would change and change;
and, higher, to the cloud that would mean this greater change,
swooping against the yellow ball of the sun.

As if through a shield of thin glass,
there was the further drone of the bomber whereby,
you said, "One day the world will be lost,"

and the bitter joke, I understood,
be on those of us who all these seasons
have played at discourse.
"Where did you go?"
So the world will ask.

The Light Going Down

The worms crawl in, the worms crawl out,
The worms play pinochle on your snout . . .
      My daughter and the schoolfriend who looks like her,
tuneless and cheerful, repeat the old ditty on Death—
pale Music Master who has not yet entered
the mind to insist on the tune.

They can't imagine what it will be
to recall from somewhere back not knowing the Master.
      I can. And go on imagining:
how would it be to go on living
backwards always, beginning
with Death? To rise from his recital room
in censure and pain, born of undying?

How brief the time
before one cast aside the cane, the crutch, and walked
      ever more into the upright,
and to hell with the Bingo, the card games!
One would feel the cloth swell taut
again over arm and thigh
and groin. A backing to bloom.

One's lifemate, assuming such good fortune,
would grow in this version more easy with every moment
      to comprehend and to love with abandon
till it seemed the two of you lay
pooled in the sweat of intimacy
forever. How would that be,

such comfort before the tears
(so useless for years) that poured
        at oddest hours, at slightest slights?
Then a horde of children hurtling (though ever more slowly)
beside you back to school, to the moments of flood
as your first love told you love had faded
before the early words of ardor sank in the playground ruckus.

Then a drawn-out unlearning
of word and figure, the telling of time.
        By now Eternity must loom,
especially summers, the elders below
chewing their words and foods on a creaking porch,
night locusts calling back another daytime.

Life must drag, everlasting,
each year a larger fraction,
        a term you no longer had the meaning of . . .
Imagining, one saddens
at the prospect of Love unraveled
and the slow unknowing

of Death, whose tenor had husked one's every testament
of affection and anger,
        until one lived oneself back past ditty
and farther. Through Mother Goose,
nonsense rhyme, to the wordless

wail of straightforward desire
as one wormed one's way to the Woman's belly,
the light going down,
and yet one knew,
from back somewhere,
how quiet it would be, how comfortless, there.

Making Sense

A tatting of wings this morning
broke silence, and dream:
a spider tethered a wasp to a mullion.
I tried, failing,
to resist my own translation—
Just as the field growth arrays
itself in summer seed fringe, it seems,
each thing in its way
begins to prepare
for winter, inside and out.
The kingdoms below us all season
have eaten and given
themselves to be eaten without
remark or record, have known fears
and lusts but not
as a man might know them:
as nooses
mounted the wings in a silken
skein, to spider and wasp,
there occurred
perhaps some version
of *Here is an end*
to all this.
Don't call it neurosis.
Their vibrations
were routine,
professional, unlike those
of a man,

one who sees how the knuckles of one hand
have turned to white onions,

and picks at his food, and
looks out the windows
through the light
spare rain.
He is inside.
Try to project
him seated there as the panes
begin with the night
to close off the pond, barn, corn piece, the last few
nighthawks slicing the last few
ephemerids from air.
As the glass collects
the dark and dew
and reflects
his small sequestered dwelling's contents
back upon him, like conscience,
or simple consciousness,
try to picture him there.
Try to imagine him try
to make nothing
of all this, to make sense
of his day, his situation,
by making outward sense
an alternative to meditation:
sight, the great turtle
he confronted when, at dawn, he pried
the hatch of his well,
and deeper in, the gutted carp in the pool;
by noon, he could *smell*
wine in the wind off windfall apples
where late-laid larvae will die;
touch, in late afternoon,
when the lame hand brushed a spit bug's drool;
the bug's unlikely whistle
will do for *sound*,
heard before supper; for *taste*,
his recall
now of an odd flavor like charcoal
in the scarred skin over his late wife's

late left breast.
For all of which the word is *Trouble*,
trouble, trouble! Not a growth from
the ground, but the ground itself
of self, which will not leave
all this alone.

I want the old man's grief
to be the winter-silent pain
of the body alone.
I want the old man older than I
to lend authority.
I want him to have learned by the end
of all this to make sense
no more than sense.
But see the hand
tense, like something that wants to take flight.
The spider has long since
retreated into sleep,
the wasp hanging
drugged in his casing.
Without comment.
Forever quiet.
But listen.
The old man will speak.
He is inside.
He will go on speaking,
I fear, into the night.

Tough End

There is no place without them,
these scourges of sense and mind. Always
on the farther reach of some divide.
When we had trains, we'd say
the other side of the tracks.
Now it's *across the brook,* or *past the Town Land,*
or *over the mountain.*
                        We call our own Tough End,
though its function of marking
an end is vague:
the middle of nowhere, and not
a finale of anything physical. Almost like dreams
to us, these dirt yards thronged with tires,
one painted white containing
the ghostly stalk of some crude flower,

                        like a far-gone drunk,
somehow still standing, poking through ashen snow.
And next to it a fridge in trance, or a dryer,
among the car and pickup wrecks.
A kind of domicilic
code of dress, everywhere honored that's country—
I've seen it in Illinois, in Georgia, in the dust-
thrashed hamlets of Canada's grain states,

                        south and north. All you need is a border.
Redneck baroque: platoons of bound and scrawny
hound-mix dogs that quake,
free-running poultry, and inside, children
who also shiver, dirty and doughy and bruised
denizen genies of the canted trailers,

sheds, or whatever. (I could tell you
of tin-can cabins, piano-crate porches,

                    but you've seen them too . . .)
The realm not only of style but also of story.
We speak the tales we know about our Tough End
in our bars, so cool and quiet, so clean, and so
unlike their yowling honky-tonk dives
named *Fuzzy Duck*, or *Breakdown Alley*, and such,
or called by their owners' brusque singular handles:
Duke's. Dick's. Pat's. Pete's. Jake's. Joe's.

                  As if in contest,
we make up our fables, each invented to top
the other, we tell them well and with rising passion,
as if we were participants
in all their outrage so long as we keep on talking,
Tough End a kind of muse's haunt
and each of us a bard.   Is it a realm of demons?
Or just the plastic stuff

                  of whatever we fashion,
sitting so. We go there—over the line—in mind
alone. Each of us knows the legends:
Gyp Smiley's store of arms
discharging itself into ceiling and sky
as his cabin blackened, the firemen afraid
to leave their trucks. Or Horace Tutt's
manner of punishing children—cigar burns,

                    scalding water, or furious shoves
from hayloft to ground.
Or each of the four Hyde brothers
in celebration of Independence devouring
a fresh-killed fawn.
The legends get old and banal,
and so we chuckle, laugh, howl, grimace, strain, flush
with labor of vision and imagination—

their wars, their murder & mayhem,
unspeakable erotics behind the veil
that Tough End draws about itself like haze
that gathers over their coal and wood stoves,
over broken wall and burning roof and prodigious unlawful feast.
Or like that curtain of rage
its citizens close on themselves as they go
—wine-sick, tobacco-hoarse—incredibly

back before we rise every day
to labor in mill, road, woodlot, field.
The closest we come to such heat is delicious frenzy
in our narration. When the spell is done,
we shake our heads,
and wish them all in hell,
as if . . .
as if we wished Tough End would vanish,

and we might live without them.

Leonora's Kitchen

After, and for, Eric Larsen

Imagine we do not know that she was so young,
that she encountered a sudden illness and fell,
gone out to the hen coop to gather eggs
for Sunday night's light supper.
The men and her boys are in town.
In the simple kitchen, the radio stutters with lightning
that flashes far off, near the station.
On the table in the middle of the room
stands a colander of beans,
red tomatoes that sweat on the oilcloth's design,
the cloth translucent
in every crease, it has been there so long.

The light is peculiar,
as if some realist painter had found a method
with light that holds the painting's mystery.
The scene can't yet be informed
by any particular pathos—
we haven't learned she lies out there,
the white hens walking idly near her,
stepping now and then across her ankles.
We cannot yet be moved to picture
one of them perched for a time on the swell of her hip,
cocking its head, spreading its meager
feckless wings and jumping down.

And the kitchen itself: it seems to do nothing
but replicate the kitchen in any house
of the country working poor,
framed as it is by porch pillars, bowed,
a floor bowed up,
a ceiling down.

The light is the apparent light of southern
Illinois on any of fifty or sixty
humid evenings, from far away
the flashes of heat.
Soon the moths will tattoo the screens,
beige on rust. She hasn't been discovered,
so the fact that she was young, was pretty and decent,
cannot mean anything yet,
if in fact it will ever mean anything.
We can't imagine in this moment
the room illuminated by anything

like that aura said to rise off the spirit rising.
Yet somehow, still, it is radiant,
and moves us, though unmoving.

Horn

You always named it
the long way for some reason:
shell of a conch,
syllables that scanned
like *son of a bitch*,
though it was only
as angry as you
ever got. Not very. No,
Father: sad. Sad, then still;
and I can't tell you how
much sadder sounding now.

You blew, it mourned
something, it wound
through secret paths
that I and my brothers—all
living then—had made
like qualifications
in the syntax of a man
reluctantly becoming
a realist. It knew
no abbreviation,
but tongued each
leaf, each stone
as it cozened us home.

We would come home slow, though,
for it wasn't the porch bell's
paratactic clamor,
expletive of terror:
Death! Drowning! Fire!

All rare
in recollection, though each
has been spoken for later.
An apparently casual
call, unchildlike, summons
to bed or meal, incidentals
in a lengthy period. We ambled
therefore, pausing
to imagine fatal
copperheads on ledges, staring
at the high ridge
with its flecked aura
of buzzards, nudging
a great toad, trying out
new risky words . . .

Let me render the sound. I can.
It held even then
the pain we feel
when we must
turn to what we have
no choice but to turn to.
Resignation's
utterance, born into us,
inflection alone
remaining to be
recalled and apprehended. Not
the percussive of lust
or catastrophe, not
the quick announcement,
midnight
phone call, bowel-shivering news
of a lover's unfaith, not
the heart-freezing
instant of diagnosis
but protracted
unease for which
the diagram is there

from the start, and on which
we gradually heap
our meanings, as flesh avails
itself of the articulate frame. Not
the hiss of the snake,
then, but as if
—in the ear's eccentric funnels—
his sound were the echo
of his body's shape,
near comatose on the bone-
warming rocks of noon.
Or the buzzard's oritund
glidings spelled
lethargic long vowels:
"Come HOME, Come HOME . . ."
Or the toad's pace
determined the meter
of our steps
homeward to the low
windings of the shell.

Not, therefore, shock
but circumlocution
of somberer fear:
slow homing,
meandering and glissando
of the conch's husk
the muddled signals of young
nemesis borne into later life
and named: vagueness,
collapse of margins, clarity
absent as night
comes on.

As night came on that night
when you beckoned
over and over,
but each time it seemed
from a different quarter,

as if you had entered the shadow—
flesh of the night-
jar whose call
imprecisely parses woods
and meadows, so is a dream
that shifts just
as you reach its stop.

Some knowledge
it may have been that stopped you
from clattering the bell.
The reluctance of summer
light in its dying? Awareness
of what we would later
plead? "We were trying . . ."
Easy sentence, come to be juxtaposed
now, as I put the horn
to my lips, blow
into it forty angry years,
and all they've cost: obscenity,
imperative, then the wailed
feckless interrogative
summons. And still,
you are lost.

The Return: Intensive Care

In memory of David Field

I felt for the button. . . .
There's a circle of perpetual occultation
at the depressed pole
within which stars never rise,
and at the elevated one, one of apparition
from which they never fall.
I used these facts
to figure the limits of my situation
—mine? or was it yours?—
as again I came back.

Where was I? . . .
I thumbed the button for your floor.
It lit.
Suddenly, I thought,
everywhere there are circles,
as in some new weather or fashion:
the breasts both of a young farm girl
and, sadder, of a fat old orderly
riding up beside me;
the elevator's orbicular light bulbs;

and, the color of linen,
each drop of snow the night before,
big and round as a saucer—
a night such as we persist in
calling a freak, though it isn't
anything more than the cycling back of things
too cursedly familiar.

Yes, though it was spring,
though it was April,
the moon had worn a great wet halo.

Signifying what?
Why look up
the facts on charts?
How often in history
has everything happened!
The nurse again wheeled away
your tray with its apple, untouched,
and two dark plums
which precisely matched,
in color and conformation,

the raccoon rounds
of valor and of exhaustion
through which your eyes peered,
brighter, still, than any planet.
O Jesus Jesus Jesus Jesus!
inwardly I cried,
to me the word
recurring like any old habit.
Poor stately Jew, forgive the helplessness
that enforced my genteel outward mode

as you lay there,
my small-talk Yankee palaver
of mercilessness in Mother Nature—
buds in remission,
pathetic birds
spiraling up from the sheeted roads
as if—I surmised—nothing now remained
but vertical migration.
I dropped my eyes. All else, anything
that I might have been moved to say,

anything that might have reached to the heart
of what we may or may not be
here on earth

to do or serve, dismayed
and frightened me.
I couldn't speak
of anything beyond the trivial,
by horror of risk held back,
by horror of saying something
even more banal.

You were on morphine.
You who for the length of this evil illness
had never complained
but had made for yourself a figure
—*Look to the light,*
or *Don't try to cling* . . .
Shy of prayer,
desperate with my own feckless
impulse to speech, at length I hung
as if in mid-air

as the dark outside
began again its round.
All so cursedly dignified!
At length, in the distilled absence of sound,
I recalled my *why why why why why!*
at the death of my small terrier.
What a petty thing to remember!
And yet perhaps those yelps
when I was so young
were the only eloquence possible.

As was perhaps the gentle rejoinder
(she had seen more than I)
of my mother's mother:
Revelation helps.
There in the hospital,
lacking for words to tender,
I had recourse to fashion.
Forgive me, I nattered;
then left, once more pushing the button;
then lifted my eyes,

searching a sign of perpetuation.
Would it do any good to tell you that I cried?
There were stars, or there were none,
from wherever it was I stood.
There was, or there wasn't, a moon.

Sereno

Month when my cord to the womb was cut, yet almost hot
this wind, all strung with ducks, with old-squaw, bufflehead,
and whistler. And the ones I'm after—high,

The clever blacks, who stretch their necks, and circle, and light
out of my range for good. There was a time
this might have prompted anger, and anger, self-contempt:

What was I doing here, blue feet and fingers blocks like wood,
the very moisture of my eyes iced over, and icebergs in my blood?
My blood flows easier with age, the rage to question

Faltering. Like useless thoughts, the trash birds strafe my blind.
My poor dogs whine: why does the gun stay silent?
Because, as I can't tell them—because I simply watch

The nobler ducks catch whiteness off the sun,
which grows these days each day more rare,
and the bay's best blue. Parade of change.

The wind from the north is warm, is wafting
forgiveness here. To noble and ignoble.
Here on Frenchman's Cove on a spit of land, and blinded,

In this strangely torpid season I forgive
the bullies and the bullied, everyone and -thing
who wants to live, that wants to live,

The chasers and the chased:
the killer put to death today by Pentothal injection,
Charlie Brooks in Texas;

I forgive the injectors;
I forgive the intractable shyness of all secrets,
like the ducks that stay far out of range.

I forgive all beings in their desperation:
murdered, murderer; mothers, fathers wanting something
the children they bring forth can't give;

Myself for my own childhood cruelties—
the way I taunted Nick Sereno
(*serene*, a thing that neighbor never was,

Dark hungry victim, bird-boned butt of my deceptions . . .
the time I decoyed him out onto the raft
and cut him loose, and jumped.

I cut the frail hemp tether, and off he drifted, quacking fear).
And I forgive the fact that cruelty can circle:
grown, he paid me back one night in a steaming gin mill.

O, this balm of sun!
As if a lifetime's bruises might be balmed.
O, that summer would at last outlast the things to come!

Out on the flooding shellfish beds the scoters pinwheel,
as if in fun and not in search of food.
I can even forgive the fighter pilots flying

Low as harriers across the headland.
They flush the drifting blacks in fear toward me.
In the hot breeze, I can count their single feathers,

Black and blue as birth,
with a seeming whiteness underneath.
Again my sweet-souled dogs look up, perplexed.

They champ their still undulled white puppy teeth.
There is more to all of this than I allow.
Here, in this paradox of weather—

Here for now I let things go,
the mind as light as light upon the wind,
as if here changed and changed into an answer.

Dusk

What do I know? Random birds. The trees.
I've split old cedar for the backyard fireplace:
in April I and my eight years' daughter made it,
our mortar so loosely mixed I remember it ran
out under the mold—in spite of my efforts to hold it—
whose wood now kindles the purposeless fire I burn.
Intent on book or doll inside, the girl
is silent. Shadowed, I stand out here alone.

Not quite. I lay a split of birch on the coals,
heartwood from two trees I couldn't save,
the roots all ruined; like pages off-white with age,
the paper bark curls back on itself in the heat.
There rise in smoke the gestures of vanished friends.
There in the clashing plaids of cap and shirt
is one who makes that odd toss, underhand,
building a fire as he goes. I imitate it.

Or try, as I have tried for years, and fail.
What is lost? Don making ready the coffee,
George and I kicking those little holes
of conversation in sand, our hunger sated,
belts let out. An ignorant boy of twenty,
I inwardly chafe at the way they study the flame,
the older others. George has arms like cable
strung to the knotted hands with which he points:

at the head of the lake, a barely discernible eagle.
Don shuffles the kettle. His spectacles glow.
The canoes run up on the beach can be hauled down,
and then, I think, God knows where we might go! . . .
Those boats were light as steam and green as lawn,
where my broadleafs faintly shine in the perfect calm,
smoke from the fireplace now a seamless line,
and I the dull bourgeois I would have despised:

I putter, I prune the trees, I weed the flowers.
Here of an evening in fall I'm satisfied,
sad and dumb. Everything is so ordered!
The day birds warbling good-bye, the evening ones
as yet unheard. I hear alone the implosions
and curious coos, inside, of our nursing infant.
A log shifts, fumes, brings tears, through which the children's
swing set, yesterday's project, glints. Time.

Time will set the concrete. The seats will be hung.
At last my daughter will climb and sway upon them,
and the baby at length. How various is pain,
how randomly shaded with joy. The single salute
of the thrush; the dove at dusk like a breathy flute;
an owl's interrogations. The dooryard darkens
and covers my trees. The ash, the hornbeam, pine.
Such mystery here, that smoke should be the constant.

Midway

He asked him, "Do you see anything?"
And he looked up and said, "I see men;
but they look like trees, walking."
Then again he laid hands upon his eyes;
and he looked intently, and was restored,
and saw everything clearly.
  —Mark 8:23–25

January.
The hours after midday are coming
back, there is time
to climb from home
to height of land for the broader vision:
north and east,
Mount Moosilauke,
its four rivers of snow conjoining;
directly west,
the little town
on the highway, all its citizens
without a doubt
preoccupied
with matters they find as grave as any;
and all around,

the traffic of beasts,
invisible now, great and tiny.
A pregnant jumble,
near and far,
then and now, in a time of year
stormy and frigid,
but I have sweated,

146

stripped to the waist, it has been so clear.
The dead have been dead
it seems so long,
and yet their ghosts are perched on every
branch above me,
cloaking themselves
in the rising vapors from my body,
the day's sole clouds.

Deep in the Sunday
village, forlorn, the sound of swings
in the empty schoolyard
clinking against
their cold steel standards, like diminished
steeple bells:
ten o'clock's
sparse service was over hours
ago. My father
lays hands on my sight
up here, and friends, and my furious brother,
who at last seems calm.
The night is losing
its sovereignty, it will not be
overlong

before it loses
its winter boast, "Come out with me,
come out and stay,
and you'll be a corpse."
The crickets, partridge, frogs will all
come back to drum
their victory;
the whippoorwills will make their hum
and click as they mate,
the freshets will loosen;
the children, done for the year with lessons,
will elect to throng
the grassy playground . . .
The past will turn itself over, shaking
out my brother,

friends, and father,
and they will be as before, but better,
as I will be,
unless — as so often —
I'm dreaming here; unless what I sense
is just another
misty version
of lifelong longing. It's hard to say . . .
A moment ago,
I flushed a crowd
of flying squirrels, who in their soaring
out of their holes
looked so like angels
I rubbed my eyes. And what do I see?
On the far horizon

appears to be
a line of men, there in procession . . .
as darkness deepens, they look like trees.

No Sign

What can we learn from Calvin,
a God-fearing man
by his own description, but also a little insane,
as he liked to say?

You'd call him simple.
But aren't we all inclined
to believe that life revolves on radical signs?

He bought a turquoise camper,
for instance, because she was growing away—his daughter
Debbie, sixteen;
and Jimmie, eleven, was showing
hints of the adolescent estrangement coming:
the feint of a sneer,
the brows that ground together,
feet that shuffled. Now, thought Calvin, or never.

Something to hold us
at least for a while together.
The longer Calvin looked, the brighter it seemed,
the rig with its chromium trim,
its velveteen carpet,
its logo (a leaping fish)—
until at last it became Incarnate Wish,
a lust at once betokened and satisfied
without a trace of guilt,
like the craving for grace
that might yet in his life be realized . . .
Ninety a month,
after two hundred down.
His wife pretended to fume

when he drove it home,
pointing wordless to the chipped weather side
of their bungalow,
to the dent in the gravel drive
that swelled with mud. But she was the same old Lizzy
at last, and giggled.
"I know," said Cal. "I'm crazy."

The Bingo had started again at the church in May,
when they didn't need oil or wood
to heat the vestry.
The men slapped Cal on the back and shook their heads.
The women applauded
the camper's color; one said,
"Like Mary's robe." Everyone laughed. One night,
Calvin and Red
and Woody took a ride
with their beers along the country roads. They all
got sentimental,
imagined a lake in fall
way up north at sunset on Calvin's behalf:
trout on the surface;
through an oxbow, the last
pillars of sun on the water; the wild loons' cackle.
"I can smell the fried fish as they sizzle,"
said Red, and friendly Woody—crude as ever—
imagined the family
"happy as hogs in manure."

Cal dropped them off and drove himself home on air.

You can't help wishing
the whole thing ended there.
It seems almost unnecessary to say
that things did not shape up exactly that way:
Debbie's a logger's mistress;
Jimmie, the boy,
is a dynamite cap of trouble.

Perhaps we should skip the intrigue,
and should keep from saying that Calvin was nuts to believe
that he could ever carry out his purpose
— bringing the family together —
with something so rootless.
For the Lord knows Calvin was rough enough on himself.
He took the camper's corrosions
as moral rebuff.
Heaven was now and forever hopeless, beyond him.
You wouldn't think
he could be so damned despondent.
Everything signaled shame: that dirty gaping
ravine in the mud,
the scars on his house's clapboard.
Calvin resorted to weeping
when he looked at Lizzy,
her hair and features fading,
the stay-at-home appearance of her clothing.

Until at last
one morning the parson selected
these words from the Gospel of Mark for his sermon's text:
"Why does this generation seek a sign?"
Whether or not
the preacher had Calvin in mind,
Calvin heard it that way.
He thought of Debbie:
what bonded him
together with her? with Jimmie?
"Truly I say to you no sign will be given"
— the Gospel quoted Jesus — "to this generation."

If there's a lesson here,
perhaps it's one
that occurred to Calvin then. It came to him
not like Revelation,
a flash of force,
but plain and simple: things will take their course.

Telescope

Light projected lifetimes ago
from farthest stars is arriving now
here where my poor house moans
on its chilling sills and stones;
and where I—quieter, sleepless,
with only my half-blind dog for witness,
everyone else in slumber—
stand silent before such wonders.
I know alone, and inexactly,
the inexact science of memory.
A man who studies things to come
for livelihood tells me in time
there will be a lens which, pointed back
to earth, may show us all our past,
even to our creation.
How little would be the elevation
it needed to show me the people
and places I might have considered crucial:
my young friend Michael drunkenly
hulking over his purple Harley,
rumbling murder in my driveway,
swearing against the blossoms of May
that pinkly dropped around us there
like what we might have taken for flares
of warning, if he had been less proud,
and I more equal to warning. I stood
dumb as a dog. You could call it collusion,
or guilt by reason of inaction.
With the glass I could also see the feathers
flare on a pheasant held by my father,

and the springer who cocked her head and chattered,
and wanted to hunt, and what was the matter?
Around us the last of afternoon fell
on the last stalks standing in autumn fields
as now, by word and heart, he petitioned
me for the slightest recognition.
I wouldn't hear the argument.
I had no interest in what was meant,
his words kept rising into balloons
of white, like those things you see in cartoons
above a speaker's head.
Turn the lens a hair and he's dead,
mouth stone-rigid, heart gone bust.
And oh how slightly I'd have to adjust
the telescope in order to see
the woeful host of memory,
other scenes—not all of course
of life and death—that exact remorse:
the way a guttering candle flickers
—I simply don't know what to give her—
in the importuning eye of a girl;
my runt chum Ronnie in a whirl
of agony as I refrain
from choosing him up for some childhood team;
the whirling earth a galaxy
of scene and soul and silence and need.
A word or two, not much
beyond what I said . . . or a touch—
how little it seems it would have taken
to change the times I now imagine
in which a now quiet man or woman,
myself included, would come off better.
But all these moments are fixed forever,
and such a lens no more effective
than memory, no more corrective.

From Another Shore

A toast in memory of Drayton Valentine

Cousin, I remember
the first drunk.

More than either of us
might say of many to follow.

Both of us fresh
off some new amorous

sorrow: you,
knees like river

weeds, down on the bank, chanting
"I Love You,

Peggy Sue," wretched whore
of a tune we loved,

it's true; I, past standing,
raising the stolen jug

and struggling up
words as if from under

the deep Atlantic, that one
last hit was left and did you want it.

The moon a mere scratch
on the blue-black gulf

of sky, but I could see
your eyes, and the dark skin

that would turn
still darker with booze

at the end, as you turned:
"Kill it," you said, and said, "By God

we have to find some girls!"
But only small fry

—giggling innocent town boys—came.
"God *damn*

a kid!" you cried,
giving lame chase.

Then the cosmic thick
conversation before unconsciousness

from which for years we would wake
proud and unsick, stars

cool swimmers over the pastures and lawns.
It was summer.
That dawn we felt we'd won one,

and at long last, evening
come, we bubbled

with laughter at the tiny
radio beaming the Hour

of Revival from deepest
blackest downtown, the Reverend Melvin,

Pastor, shouting,
"I, too,

was a drifter, drenched in liquor,
till something grabbed me,

turned me *around!*"
Turn to me, first friend,

and I'll tell you something
grabbed me too.

(I have friends
who say it was God,

but I don't know,
it didn't grab you . . .)

Time to go,
time to turn

the choir off, choiring triumph
that Pharaoh lay forever

still, his eyes gummed shut with salt.
Time to cruise

the asphalt, steaming,
violent-loined, with no one to love

except each other.
You pointed a steady

finger at the dial:
"Enough of these losers.

Kill it." The crackling
tapered off

like remotest storm.
One kills so much:

friendships, time,
the moist erotic hungers

of an August, wives, lives.
I seem to survive, and thought

I'd killed off you.
I have a couple of kids. One plays

"We Are the Champions,
My Friend." Loud and louder,

day after day.
I love him. Friend,

gone downriver
a decade, and I

turned back to dry land,
I don't know why. Somewhere

the woman you damn
near drowned in grief is raising

a daughter, my cousin,
once removed.

I don't know her name,
but think

it has Victoria in it,
or Victory.

Let's call it Victory here.
For you. For me.

Annual Report

For my wife

What reason to begin and end just here
—in May, the woods still rank with late gray snow
through which the jets of adders'-tongue will show
before too long—this song about our year?
O plenty, there is plenty in this month
that marks the twelve gone by since our son's late birth:
encased; released; prostrate; now he uprears
himself on this rich festival of earth.
Tiny grace note to you who freight with grace
this spot, and yet a miracle of growth.
May this report be my attempt to pray
he'll grow like you, and all will. May the throat
deliver words all virginal, like his.
May they seem apt as his by way of praise:

My love, what in this calendar is worst
is mine for every season. What is best,
claim for yourself; for when the infant burst
the raptor bubble of your lean long frame,
the worm that sprawls in me gave out a shriek,
a wail in his beloved Devil's name,
lament that he had found himself grown weak . . .
In June, a month of blackflies, blooms, and gnats,
you and my daughter of seven broke the ground
for zinnia, marigold. Those canvas hats
you wore, their bug-veils drooping down,
were comic then, but now in mind appear
as things of beauty too, as if there were

in God's creation nothing beautiless.
Even the insects' wry persistent drone
comes back to me as something sweet and fine.
The gray along the toothless maw of Jess,
our old retriever, seems a kind of mantle.
He lay down on the kitchen floor, and gentle
—as he was always gentle—died. July.
The dust is fled that powdered on his grave,
the single apple sapling—Northern Spy—
I planted out of season there forms pips.
O keep the worm away, I pray, a trope
that loops through boughs, the grave, the house, the lips
of sleeping kids, your own, the studded cope
of summer night. Let all of this be saved,

and August's lake: the dawns, the mists like fountains
—grays the sun transfigured. Now forever
may I see you poised in mind against the mountain
that rims the western shore. And calling weather,
the widow loon will swim into such vision,
her cry the braver plainsong to the worm's
shrill descant of self-pity. O girl bride,
I know myself gone by the middle season,
but I would die of grief not to have died
before you do. May God save all the children.
Yet may the mind recall as well the terms
by which it's meant to live in sanctity:
the world's "subjected to futility
not of its own will but by the will

of Him who subjected it in hope." Ah, still,
who can ignore the huff of tragedy
in the first fall gust? September:
the Northern Spy's gray fruit-lumps suddenly
small fires, and just as suddenly—remember?—
the child's opposing teeth, with which he bled
your tender breasts. You wept aloud, you said,
less for that pain than for the pain of knowing
perfection in those tiny rows of bone,

from which perfection now he'd be ungrowing.
As purest joy may flash in the mundane,
just so with woe. We thought of dentists' bills,
of wires perhaps, like those that his half-brother
must wear against a skewed and painful bite,

grid of metal gray across such white!
We are subjected not of our own wills.
Just now at last I've mentioned the half-brother.
Is this a telling figure? Am I half-father?
My firstborn, he who set the worm at bay
which then returned, returns. And then the daughter
sent him off. He came again. The baby
banished him once more. Can this mean I
must save myself by constant siring? Maybe,
although the beard goes gray, and slack the body.
But I was speaking of the boy, October.
Two months shy then of his thirteenth birthday,
his face and mood would suddenly turn somber
as earth when leaden autumn clouds heave over:

How I recall myself in such a season!
My father's shoulders dropping slack and round,
my mother turning mannish. The dreadful wound
and thrill of sex and self-preoccupation.
The world, just now all springtime, in a blink
a seamless, dreary, flat, and chill November.
The boy's eyes flooding gray . . . I know I think
I know his thoughts, though "thought" is not the word;
who would impute it to the self-willed member,
evil's root as much as filthy lucre,
shape- and soulmate of the filthy worm?
And yet an organ of sincerest pleasure . . .
It seems that I, in wandering mazes lost,
proceed by warring halves. Is that the cost

to one who seeks to front "futility"
as Paul construed it for the Roman churchmen?
Is "hope" its mocking earthly avatar?
Are all the impassioned songs and poems to women

made by lonely men a litany
whose hidden theme is gloomier by far
than they may think? The intercourse they beg
by way of overcoming cheerless halfness
—figured in decembral chill and fog,
not clarity nor yet true thrilling storm—
no intercourse at all? If so, we're hapless.
(I hear the faint sick murmur of the worm.)
Oh, put it off! The children all were born,

and if the sudden plunge of January,
freezing bone, suggested vanity,
didn't the sun come on to melt the gray
of rime from windows, and indeed the hills
show clearer then than ever? One could see
the valiant buds begin their yearly pull
against what seemed damnation. And can't I
—good coffee perking, infant sprawled in bed—
pull equally? Your laughter fills each room.
How do you do it? Life-love, teach me how.
"Is that," you whisper, pointing to the stairs
down which my sleepyheaded daughter treads,
"an emblem of futility and doom?"
I'll make of this whatever I allow . . .

In mind, the school bus was a mobile jonquil,
giant bud in February's gray.
Because of you, these bursts into the tranquil.
Because of you, not least of all your ear
(I have already credited your eye)
for valiant things: our neighbor said last year,
so you remind me, of his rabbit hound,
"He's got so old he has to lean against
a bank to howl." The hound is in the ground,
the neighbor too, so soon our time is spent.
And yet the two survive by dint of will,
theirs then, yours now. I give our pup a pill
to quell his worm. (If only a pill quelled mine!)
As the children's school bus ambles off, it shines.

March, as fits the proverb, came like lions
and out it went, all lambs, at least in color:
a late snow powdered every inch of lawn,
but when we looked around was gone. A flower
—lily—poked its tongue beneath a gray,
steaming hulk of stump, around which played
springtails, or snowfleas as we call them here.
Imagine them, such tiny signs of life
against all odds, about to end their year,
as we shall too, my very perfect wife.
Vermicular, they seem, but innocent
as those great moths that bear a question mark
upon each wing, come softly in the dark,
their question, maybe, Why not be content,

why not affirm by will what is? In April,
they clustered thick as fleece upon the screens,
the evening dark itself grown soft. My dreams
of piercing through the gray of mystery
on earth seem idle. Now, the year's full circle:
cased blossoms bursting from the apple tree,
the prostrate dog now grass, one son a man,
a daughter who like you grows beautiful,
an infant who has found a way to stand,
the worm entombed as if beneath a mountain,
this spot of ground a fête of resurrection,
since what is hope if not futility
for moments stood on end? My love, it's May,
first month of our obscure divinity,

creator, creature, riddle, lover, maid.

5

From *Prayer for the Little City*

(1991)

Prayer for the Little City

6 January

Hushed plane, the pond.   Ice fishers' lights.   Still little city.
Men hug their whiskey   jugs inside   as they loiter among
whiffs of bait,   potbelly smoke,   sock wool and sweat.

Laconic chat: an idle joke;   or goddamn that
or goddamn this,   although such words   aren't even angry,
but ordinary.   Snowmobile roads   thread our shacks

one to another;   now and then,   Big Lou throws open
his door (like an oven's,   infernal within)   and cries to a neighbor,
"Doin' some good?"   Or dirty Duane,   the one we call

"Blackfly," will call   words much the same   and the neighborhood
will rally from silence   a moment or two,   then sink back in.
It's half past ten.   Blackfly and Lou   and all the quietened

others stay through   the darkness till dawn,   whether or not
the small smelt bite.   What *of* this town,   this bob-house crew?
What of Ben,   who's outside skimming   his ice hole's o's?

He sniffs and blows,   thinks vaguely of women,   and thinks to name
some part of their bodies   out loud across   the frozen surface:
a shout all worthless,   directionless,   a shout all shoddy

with platitude,   devoid of embrace,   containing nothing,
not even longing . . .   at least for sex.   Just part of a mood
and situation   much at odds,   it   might be imagined,

with a hopeful season,   season of gods,   of resolution
to start anew.   Outside, the flags   on their planted poles
in the utter chill   are utterly slack,   betraying no

visionary   prey down under   to clasp our lures.
The dullness is pure.   No signs, no wonders,   no mystery . . .
except it be   the care with which   all night men linger,

as if in prayer   for a novel fish,   or a novel way
by which to address   some thing they're feeling.   Surely this is
part of what holds us   under crude ceilings   beaded with pitch,

amid this fetor   with speechless friends.   Surely, surely
a sense that early,   before the dawn   (or sooner, or later)
our flags will all   at once, together,   tremble and shimmy.

Epiphany   —o bright palaver!   o every hole
a yodel of steam!   So runs our fancy   in the absence of sound
in this merest of towns,   although our shanties'   very beams

of light seem bored.   O little city,   we think, it's cold;
city, how still,   how still we see thee.   Still, the stars
go by above,   even here,   and still may love

embrace the year.

Two Chets

Let us face it.
Life is stranger
than our inventions, being the ground
thereof, being the limit,

being the promise and instantaneous close.
We sip its baffling springs.
There I was,
just driving down

Route 22 at the corner
where it dips below Calvin's house.
No matter that you don't know him;
this doesn't mean a thing.

I was simply following Chet
toward the river.
I knew him by the way he cocked
his head, and his silly swordfish hat.

As if he had ever seen the ocean!
I knew his truck,
and how he rode ever so slowly
(may God bless

such instances of decency!)
because he knew himself
driving drunk as usual.
On the decline,

he looked in his mirror
and made his customary little sign
—not quite a wave—with two fingers.
He sat small in the pickup's chassis,

which was small itself against Mt. Bower,
granite moraine,
bleak, dismal,
though I know it foot by foot, from its foot

across the narrow lane
by the Andersons' diner
up to where it's nothing
but slag and skinny pine.

(From there you can see back this way
to Mt. Held and the right-wing governor's farm.
If there were nothing
else to do so, his example would warn—

Never say *simple* or *simply*.)
I felt the usual comfort
of being known by others, knowing them.
I didn't think to be scared of lyrical faith,

to be glad I didn't have it
nor, quite, its absence. Then
along came this Chevy S-10.
I could see its driver's empurpled face,

he drove so slowly up the other lane,
splashing the minuscule puddles.
I saw the absurd long bill of his cap,
like a round-point spade.

I saw its familiar angle,
and the head's as well.
Both of us kept on moving,
but here's the little part I want to tell:

It was Chet, Chet waved,
and when I looked back
to where I was going,
that other Chet ahead of me was gone

without a trace.
Not that Chet is anything much.
Not that I am either.
Yet ahead there was nothing

but the insignificant town
against the mountain,
whose freshets ran athwart each other
down the famished and ravaged face,

falling, falling out of the dark scrawny
evergreen bushes.
Don't remind me
how low this ranks among the wonders,

how trivial it is, how slight
the slender waters' singing rushes,
whatever I may have imagined.
Let me ask you, stranger:

what are those flashes
when something happens and unhappens
all at once, and you see life,
its starts, its odd reverses?

Questions of Empathy Way Upstate

Can we guess that this ground is québecois?
Is that why its heavy rocks are gathered
dead center, and not in Yankee walls?
Do crops of these pasture rocks grow nightly?
Does anything happen here that matters?

Can we feel if the farmer feels despair?
That isn't—is it?—very likely.
Just now can we guess that he's looking through
his window toward that shrine out there?
That now he mutters, *Tout foutu?*

Is it really a bathtub, stood on end?
Can we guess that the farmer painted it
a hue that seemed appropriate—
angel blue, as the label said?
Does Baptiste moan, *She's dead, She's dead?*

Can it really be a grot for The Virgin
—plastic figure, suction-cup base?
What is the ground of this, our vision?
Can we see it under the locust trees?
And do those tatterdemalion leaves

anneal themselves to it in storm,
pale, like chalkings of grounded birds?
Why do we call this man Baptiste?
Do even plastic features grow worn?
Are they as heavy and worn as his,

now that his little Louise is gone?
For him, has too much happened here?
Lou-Lou, Lou-Lou, est-elle disparue?
Does heavy rain fall? Does he mumble a prayer
at our Bathtub Lady of Angel Blue

for everything to rise on air?

Pietà

It is not any single version
that moves me so, but all: great Buonarotti's
no more than the one I bought as if to mock it
      on its smarmy Venetian postcard whose cake-pink Virgin's

tears bring me tears. That He is grown
(as much an adult, you could say, as she)
is part of what weighs on me.
      But who's it *for*, this grief of mine,

this mourning? The fact of touch. And the mystery—
sublime or vulgar, sobbing or stoic,
the two are ever other. Crude, heroic,
      distracted, whatever: in every rendering I see,

so other. Of course there's sadness that a mother
should posture with her blasted seed, but fineness,
surely, too. I wonder if Kliney,
      my oddly named and fated brother,

before the hemorrhage fully blacked his brain,
felt some such mother touch.
Once he'd left the breast, there wasn't much
      by way of laying-on of hands

between those two. This poem
assigns no blame to either party. I
am the one who writes it, I who've shied
      as much as he from home,

as much beyond her reach.
Or no, not quite as much. I'm still alive.
I don't know how I've reached this dim surmise
      that as the pale tube leached

its useless glucose nurture from a sack
and the EEG's thin scribble flattened out
she dropped the bright steel rail and put
    her fingers to his face — but that

is the thing that touches me beyond all reason.
That, and the countervision, that as in life,
in death as well the two were stiff
    and formal, blood between them

too much, and years, and that the Anglo-
Saxon sequesters passion out of sight.
Does everyone sometimes? That night,
    dazed farmers, as they angled

headstrong herds to fold, may well have mumbled
clichés on weather, games, and levies,
like us when things, as the saying goes, get heavy.
    And heavy they'd been. Earliest miracle

in fact was maybe that Mary was enlightened
— in every sense the word can carry —
enough to hold him there, to parry
    the nuisance thrusts of insects, cleanse him, frighten

away the innocent rubbernecking kids.
Miracle of grace — or was it courage?
The funeral lacked all cant or flourish.
    You sat erect there, Mother. What you did

three days before in the darkened ward
I've never learned. This is a kind of guessing,
maybe a way of asking.
    To hold a ruined man who's yours

as husband, friend, or lover
can never be . . .
It is the unthinkable *notion* that touches me,
    as much your flesh as the ruined brother.

The notion and the posture, and he within it,
manchild, or maybe not at all.
As I might be. Pity. *Pietà*.
    Mercy. I could think to want it.

173

For the Solitary

So that's why they've said he's thinner. Cancer.
Now it sounds like a pun, and meaner,
What someone remarked years back about him:
"He isn't much. You'll barely see him."
That's all I was told, latecomer, stranger,

But that he'd always yearned for Alaska,
Had coveted its mystic scale,
Who lived on trifling Sutter's Knoll
Beside his stone-and-vegetable patch,
Who paints today his shoebox shack,

Out of hiding at last, in bright fall air.
I spy. I wonder what brings him here.
I wonder if he's concluded his hamlet
Contains far more than he ever imagined—
Acorn, antler, ridgeline, rock,

Great-fledged turkeys with swollen crops,
Grays, profuse in this late November
And variegated as blues in midsummer,
Black marble of night, dawn's poppy sun.
I might go on. He might go on

To apply exorbitant ornamentation
As planets school toward winter positions,
And spring's grown broods leave tracks in gravel,
And ducks on the sloughs churn upward, startled
By their own splendor of plumage, it seems,

And frost-emancipated seeds
Troop to ground or stream in cascade.
As things prepare to go spare they explode
Or shine: the fatted cattle's ordures,
The lapidary mounds of fodder,

Jet flies drifted by southern windows,
Worms in the dark of their ruinous tunnels.
At daybreak the brilliant roosters cry:
Any day now! Any day!
And yet, I see, for all of that,

He chooses a dim, transparent shellac.
O, if only he would have it,
His circumstance might be Alaska —
Vast, obscure, particular.
Is the dark of the pine groves any darker?

Oak bark is nuanced with jadelike green.
Something perhaps in me alone —
A stranger now as much as ever —
Desires a luminous closing figure.
You'll barely see him will be *you didn't.*

He *isn't much* will be *he wasn't.*

Late Season

This was the last I'd trouble the ducks this season:
there'd be skim-ice on the sloughs
and later, snow come down from Canada, horizontal.
There might be some luck, a little . . .
no, more. It was already there, beforehand:
dirt road near dawn, canoe
snubbed in the pickup's bed,

and in my lap the great good head
of my dog, the blood in his graying muzzle
a pulse in my leg as we bucked the ruts.
And, come down from a Canada even farther,
music, local notices, news of the weather—
the radio's early report. I imagined the struggle
of a farmer there. Up like me. *Good mutt,*
I whispered. I scratched

the retriever's neck.
It was warm.   Reception good.   The farmer leaned
in mind into winds that they say
can straighten a tow-chain out behind a tractor.
I liked driving tractor-slow, imagining that weather.
Plenty of time. Down here, whatever the wind,
I could count for now on a milder day.
I was forty-five.   I liked how the AM signal

said something about what it was to be fuddled,
or rather how static fell away when your object was clear:
getting from house to barn and back in a gale;
getting the decoys out before you froze;
getting into the proper kinds of clothes
to meet a day.   Getting it right.   A cold time of year,

but for now I was snug behind the wheel,
and already I could envision

the redleg black duck blown down and past in migration,
the reach of a wave from the farther shore of the river
toward me, where I'd sit, alone but for the dog.
Wave like a single important announcement.
A blind of fragile reeds, and all around it
the signs of how we must seek to save forever
what we receive of what goes by: a buck
who has left his ghostly track in slush and mud;

gleam of low sun in old blood;
spent shells, drifting clumps of insubstantial feather,
gone in a moment, abiding in the mind;
feel of a dog companion's eager breathing
turned to frost on your cheek, then melting to nothing.
Later the awful snow would come to the river,
and later the careful blind no longer stand,

nor dog, nor duck, nor I, nor Canada farmer.

Manifest

Litany: winter walk

In evergreens, wind-riven,
     whose blaze orange wounds
     at limb and crown certify passion;
In the mitten-wool taste
     of snow you scoop to your mouth
     because—so you imagine—you thirst;
In illogical woodpeckers' laughter,
     in their swooping flight,
     that suggests assertion crossed by doubt;
In rough-frozen rims of tracks
     the animals left in the dark preceding
     nights, whose meaning needs no glossing;
In the hue of a beech
     —neither quite somber gray
     nor placid blue—that teases all sight and belief;
In the way this sun at solstice
     jumps up from the hill
     and asks no reading, but affirmation in the chill;
In the ermine who fought the owl,
     resisting negation:
     alone now, scarlet in snow—conspicuous, stiffened;
In the steam of your coffee at dawn,
     pale testimony to addiction, harmless,
     perhaps more so than others you want;
In one long-damaged knee
     whose cartilage resists your walk, and warns
     against a mock tranquility;

In the bland and sweet obedience
        of your dogs, which raises questions
        that touch on your worthiness, competence;
In the warmth (to which you'll return)
        of shelter, so easily canceled should your fuel
        withhold its fire—a residue of the sun;
In fire, that has the power and glory
        of "the things that have been made," as St. Paul saith,
        commanding faith, however airy;
In warmth and shelter and fire,
        to which of course you will return,
        for which you are whetting desire;
In desire, whose quenching is life
        and death, as poets used to say—
        by enjoinder and designation: *husband, wife;*
In this cheery fall of siskins
        to an earth that you'd thought barren: in their number,
        that may be somewhere counted, their busyness;
In their vanishing
        —before you can count them yourself—
        that sermonizes vanity;
In the far waw of a power saw
        that binds on a softwood's sap, congealed:
        the logger swears profanely, we are not healed;
In the warming recollection of your children,
        for whose sake you pray as you can for death
        to have no dominion, that you are forgiven.

Pianissimo

Although I've claimed to know the language well,
So gentle is his call, so low—a vowel,
A breath—small wonder that its pain escapes me.

I've left behind my glasses: when he falls,
Beside a vineyard, in a field, downhill,
At first I lose him. Tiny in the poppies,

He seems a figure from some magic tale,
Flower stems the bars of his soft jail.
Can that sweet call have meant, *Signore, save me?*

Just now I might be anywhere at all,
A tourist only, from another world.
I might be hiking any other valley.

What he whispers next I can't quite tell,
Though once I claimed I knew this language well.
I think, though, every other word's *morire*.

Things seem far too still, as in some spell
Or dream in which one needs to run and fails.
I'm locked in gentle dusk in the Chianti,

The broom in bloom, whose magical sweet smell
Configures with some Angelus's bell.
At that, where might I run? I lift him gently,

Like a baby. On a ruined wall,
A lizard shows a pulse, redundant, small,
Like tickings of the watch I've left behind me,

On my holiday, with time to kill.
Only such slight fibrillations tell
He lives at all. O spell, O sweet *far niente*:

Lost to deed and word alike, I fall
Into your snares. This stillness overall
Will find his heart at last. My will betrays me.

An ox uphill lows gently from a stall.
The tiny man breathes softly still, *Signore*,
No longer, though, I think, to me at all.

Or is the word, I wonder, still *morire*?
I'm just a tourist here in the Chianti,
So much of this soft dialect escapes me.

Museum

Recalling George MacArthur and Donald Chambers

Small thunder cuts my autumn doze on the porch.
Trotting by, two thoroughbreds—skittish, slender.
Dream is at once a heavy and delicate thing.

Donald's wrinkles could hold a week of rain.
Every fall, he told me, he'd bleed his horse.
A horse's waters thicken, summering over.

Or did he say he bled her after winter?
He spoke so much, so often, I ought to remember.
He said and said and said, I wasn't there.

A horse don't mind, she didn't mind, he said.
He'd make a jutting movement into air.
You put the knife-point, quick as you could, inside.

A Belgian would barely flinch, God was his witness.
He swore the roan mare didn't care.
Only a little prick in the palate's softness.

It's America, it's 1988.
Shy, the thoroughbred pair, and thin in the leg.
Soft and bright, the rider's clothes—like mine.

Queenie, he whispered, she lowered her trunk of a neck.
Her look was almost bored, she seemed to yawn.
There stood a barrel, and blood came pouring down.

You needed to stanch it with alum right on time.
A horse was a thing you wanted not to lose.
By God you wanted a rugged horse back then.

Back then the trees got bigger than they do.
My road was just a path in the swamp, of course.
I wasn't there, repeat, not there, repeat.

You can't remember somebody now by a horse.
Not by a horse that really works, at least.
All I recall is Donald telling me of it.

Queenie, he'd whisper, repeating her name, he loved it.
You can't recall a person by a canoe.
I'm thinking now of George as well, awake.

Not a canoe you use, you really use.
You had to portage then from here to the lake.
Riverman, river of words, song singer, bard.

The only roads were tote roads then, George said.
Repeating himself, repeating, I wasn't there.
You could borrow the loan of a horse if you were tired.

A timber horse, well bled and fed, was strong.
A Belgian would hardly pay a canoe attention.
You lashed it onto a sledge and drove it on.

George and Donald were there, who now are gone.
And this may be the realm of imagination.
When the black ducks flew from the lake they covered the sun.

When a he-bear coughed in the woods, the great flanks trembled.
You threw wet trout on the garden to feed your corn.
You bled a horse in autumn, or was it spring?

Good smell of flesh and blood, hay dust in the hovel.
Even in January the flanks would steam.
Vaporous stuff of New England. Imagination.

Useless, swift, and helpless, the thoroughbreds.
Dream's domain; talk unto song; museum.
You have to make sure that too much blood don't spill.

They told me so, they laughed, they frowned, they said.
There were rocks, rapids, currents you couldn't feel.
Solid things and spectral, redundant winds.

There were widowmakers, limbs that fell without sound.
Sometimes, though, the horses seemed to hear.
Sometimes they'd bolt, and a ton of horse can maim.

That much horse is a delicate thing all the same.
So Donald always suggested, I wasn't there.
You could fix any boat you didn't completely lose.

Sometimes I lose it, even the shadow from slumber.
Canvas and cedar, ash ribs, gunwales of spruce.
Mist, recalls—Donald and George, New England.

Horses, canoes, talk, men, museum.
Thunder: wood scrap, green cloth going under.
The old men's regal faces could hold the rain.

One twitches the horse's lip, the knife jabs in.
Riders wave to me from the road all cheerful.
I think the Belgian mare's big legs will buckle.

I think we're late, and blood brims over the barrel.
Its stain is the shade of these Indian summer maples.
It's 1988, the canoe is fragile.

The spindly trot comes liquid through autumn air.
Words I repeat and repeat for George and Donald.
I say and say and say who wasn't there.

Another Autumn, And

Again the trees' loud story
                    quietens, grounded;
at roadside, tumbled foliage
                    scatters, whispers
again the world is sinking
                    into night,
and further minor
                    pastoral nullity:
the shadows lengthen fast,
                    and so on. Ended,
composition will seem
                    to have been erasure,
the whole a notebook's
                    leaf left white.

I take our little boy
                    along with me,
a two-year-old, too young
                    I think to care
about originality.
                    He kicks
a weary crackle
                    from red maples here,
pale poplars there. The way
                    the mind falls back,
falls *up*, seems both at once
                    eccentric and banal.
He kicks. You kicked. I kicked.
                    We kick the leaves.

And once these things we did
                    seemed fine and final,
seemed a turning over
                    of something new.
Father, it's '58.
                    It's been a struggle,
so you say, but now
                    it's on the rise.
I'm thinking other things,
                    but think this too.
You mean you've saved
                    your little company.
You're praising effort, family,
                    faith, and Ike.

My mind is racing:
                    I intend to write!
And you're my age, and don't
                    intend to die.
I turn to leave. I love you;
                    it is just . . .
My blond boy wants and doesn't
                    want to be
like me. I want to go
                    back to our house.
He doesn't, races on,
                    but turns to see
if I will follow.
                    I would recompose
the past and future. Now
                    I whisper, "Home."
He kicks and shouts. He turns
                    and races on.
And now I think he's growing
                    like a weed
I'd like to go and empty
                    all the graves . . .

And here the sun is low,
         and somewhere high,
and all that falls will vanish
         and abide.
And in the shadows
         he is shouting "Leaves!"

For Faith

All had a look and meaning, she remembers.
The spirals of birds—adieu—in autumn's bluster.
Sun turning shadows from gray to black, and darker.
Notes on the brittle hymnal pages, signatures . . .
Clouds, swelled in the tawny highland pastures
till they looked like snow on sand.
Gales that boded fair or ugly weather,
and the northward lake's attendant moods and colors.
Or something indoors, like wood mites fretting the rafters.

The ancient organ's keys are chilly, tan,
but they warm and even brighten under her hand.
Crackle of August grasshoppers all through the land
so loud she feared that the timothy-stubble burned.
For prelude, something noble, *forte*, grand.
The tiny choir in her mirror,
sleep in their eyes. Can she stir them still? She can.
Outside, resplendent, scarlet in Sabbath sun,
a convertible-top Corvette: it's hers, who ran

with her lucent, blood-bay mare beside her father,
riding astride in the piquant vacations of Easter:
shine of mane in the breezes; gull squawks; lather;
turf, puddle, saddlesoap, evergreen, leather;
new grass rolling in waves to mimic the water's.
Or the naked cardinal plant,
Oriental in hailstone-pearled northeasters.
Or a chirr in the pantry: the laboring separator.
And her voice, so achingly clear, that makes these over . . .

Season after season, arriving, turned:
Summer's giant evenings, late to begin
and coming like fog or scent so stealthily on,
as, playful, she hid with her restive dogs in the barn.
At C above staff, there's one odd pipe that groans.
She has been the familiar
of this organ a long long time: the stop that pretends
it is *vox humana*, the autonomous F that sounds
if you hold the leftmost pedal too far down,

or mutes itself in the tonic chord for D-minor.
So much of this depends upon the weather.
The muteness, as well, and the pallor of her father,
sprawled in mud next to a calf he'd delivered.
Staring at whitecaps through kitchen windows, Mother
wheezed in rhythm, her hands dropped listless beside her.
How throaty, the sports car's motor:
it's not, however, something she'll consider,
leaving it all behind. She raises a finger,

hoping Janette of the quavery alto will note her,
will alter a flatness; or maybe she as director
will take her part and sing it louder and drown her.
And still Janette will love her. That's the wonder.
So I think—quiet as a mime in my corner—
dreaming I understand.
Now, as the anthem follows, she starts all over.
If I'm wrong, still something rich and grand must move her
and make that light a fool could see above her.

6

From *The Blainville Testament*

(1992)

Proem: After George's Ax Was Stolen

I came back to camp at nightfall,
a scene that, wanting an object, had changed:
How old my dooryard pine had grown,
the woodpeckers having their way.
Above my lumber pile,
decay in a shimmer rose.

I said aloud, "I ought to do something."

I heard the hidden owls' redundancies,
but where was the nighthawk,
his solid bang of wing
as he fell like a heavy blade through a haze of mayflies?
Where were the mayflies?
Wood lice were turning my cabin's timbers to lace.

It was his, but he left it to me.

Far off, the last of the logging trains.
I shouldn't merely hug myself, I thought,
rocking back and forth
on this granite slab that the river slaps
and ceaselessly slaps
until one day it breaks through.

I ought to go someplace.

On this long shelf where water
expends itself as froth in the Giant Eddy
—where so often we sat while George sang
or told from his monumental store of stories
that made of life a shape:
all that motion, action!—

I sat down and wept.

Once I had saved the ax's handle
from porcupines who fretted it for salt
and didn't care to whom it belonged.
The head had such authority:
six pounds and a half of metal, forged to endure,
whatever the incidental

sallies of rust, of rain gone acid.

He'd brag on the heaps of railroad ties he could pile
in a single day,
out with ax and lantern before the dawn,
back after dark the same way,
for a whole long season
never to see his shack but under stars.

Like this one.

Air passed without resistance
through the kitchen corner
where the ax had stood for years,
used only so that my children might see
how it cleaved the staunchest stovewood
as if it were foam.

Maybe that was it. Children.

Who else would break in and take
no other thing that the world might value?
Unless it were someone else who loved him . . .
unless it were someone
who also sits just now,
things before his eyes transformed, dispersed,

as a far locomotive faintly cries,

and a boulder moon on the rise
behind a fragile shack and a gnarled pine
scatters these little starlike shapes
on ledge till it looks like a sieve—
wondering, *Where shall I go?*
wondering, *What shall I do?*

The Blainville Testament

For Mark Jarman and Robert McDowell

I remember how that canny man Montaigne
wrote that all philosophy consists
in learning how to die. Not that to tell
this tale will be my death. But I want it right.
Nor that philosophy is what I'm after;
words, rather—the way that strung together

they help things last. Or may. I put them here
because of late the spoken ones come hard,
for want of conversation and of breath.
It's how they can both take and give back shape
I love. For much that we call love attaches
to eloquence in things, if you can catch it:

Creases in a favorite pair of shoes.
A certain slant of light, as the White Nun said,
on winter afternoons. Or odors, timbres,
sounds. Whatever craves and begs translation.
Think of a favorite cup whose dents and scratches,
if you could merely find their proper order,

make runic narrative of all your mornings.
Your chimney's sibilants, whiffs of a bush.
Feel of your hand along a porch's rail.
I have a special stake in this, you see.
You'll see, that is, if I can rightly show
the things that I've attended all these years,

and more important, what they've said to me
in spite of all my neighbors' bleak assurance
that I would never comprehend this country.
"A lawyer!" so they huffed. "And from the city!"
I'm sick to death with all of that, as well
as with The Crab. And yet, although he prods,

he is a friend. Or maybe he's a she,
as the late insurance man (a lawyer, too)
lately put it: "Death is the mother of beauty,
within whose burning bosom we devise
our earthly mothers waiting, sleeplessly."
Oh, I have memorized the fine devices!

Lord knows my poor old-womanish bosom burns
and I'm sleepless here, mothering The Crab,
The Crab my mother. We get on together,
especially with the moon out there so brilliant.
We see across the meadows to The Bald Man,
and summon other forms as well—the spruces

I once knew, the barred owls crouching in them.
Hardwoods too, their shadows on the snow,
there! and there! and there and there and there!
In mind, I travel through them, breathing cool,
as I did one winter to visit Billy Fields,
six months after Blainville cut him dead,

except as a kind of allegoric figure,
referred to for the sake of local color.
If you're from here, you'll know just what I mean,
and what it's meant to me, his confidant.
But if you're not, you'll want me to explain.
And I'll oblige, since I am in no hurry,

and since I'm not yet sure whom I write *for*.
It may be I address myself alone.
Should you take interest, though, then you must hear
—as I, arrived post facto, heard—of Mark.
Town legend calls him Billy's Victim still,
a designation I'll leave you to judge.

This boy was smart, which word here signifies
something like handy, or quick to learn, or both.
He was among our first to drive a car,
the first to plumb or rig a house with light.
Others could hit a ball from plate to pond
as he could do, but only Mark would have

some slick machine down-cellar to make his bat!
He didn't drink. He didn't chew or curse,
and loved — a thing for local praise — to work.
Shiftless Brian Hart would ask him up
to his hunting camp on The Bald Man and pray for sleet,
so Mark, all cabin-feverish, would tend

whatever needed fixing on Hart's shack.
"Last fall was good," joked Brian once. "It hailed.
The roof leaked through until he patched it up
with half a shingle and seven common nails!"
Mark grinned and kicked his boot toe in the dust.
Hart's trick had been no trick. Mark wasn't fooled,

just, as always, happy to oblige.
A paragon, in brief, in every sense —
moving picture handsome, a hero's posture,
teeth that might be wrought from dearest marble,
an automatic decency. He was
model and darling both. He had a way

of knowing what to do to help a neighbor
before the neighbor knew. Especially elders.
Elsie Cammon's cow once choked to death
on a backwoods apple. (Her fence was never much,
became a local figure: a man might say
"tight as Elsie's fence" if he meant loose.

Though all was change then, still the region spoke
a language brightly eloquent of place,
of men and women working in the place,
though it was often mean, like "kind as Fields,"
or "Elsie's face is rough as a bag of hammers,"
or — as I've heard — "windy as city lawyers . . .")

Billy went that day with Mark to see
the cow put underground. No one knows why.
I whose lawyer's job it was to sort
Mark's tiny leavings—I can say at least
the darkest rumor is a fantasy:
"Murder for money?" There wasn't any money!

Whatever for, old Fields went out with Mark.
Mark had used a kind of homemade tractor
to drag the cow back farther in the woods.
He'd ploughed a hole, and meant to roll her in.
How Billy cursed and grumbled at such waste
in telling me! But be that as it may,

Mark was set to heave the poor beast in
when he dropped his brand-new watch in the brand-new grave.
(He'd had it in his shirt, according to Billy,
which struck the town as odd, to say it mildly.)
Mark jumped down to fetch it, the ground gave way,
and half a ton of beef fell in upon him.

A radical story some here still expound
was that Billy shoved the cow. "At 79?"
So I would ask. "He moved eight hundred pounds?"
"Never mind. He shoved her with the tractor."
(That he'd never seen a motor didn't matter.)
The commoner accusation, less extreme,

was that Billy sat and watched Mark bleed to death
from wounds the rib-bones made along his side.
The service that at last can fall to me
is letting Billy tell us his own version.
No one, while he lived, would ever ask it
face to face of him. And *I've* suppressed it

all these years. "A lawyer's sworn to silence,"
so I'd claim (my little irony).
For nothing I could say would make a difference.
The town already felt it was suspicious
that I was Billy's counsel at the hearing
and also settled Mark's so-called estate.

Of course who else would do such chores back then?
But there was talk. And let them go on talking
when—like all my characters—I'm gone.
I cannot care. For better or for worse,
they'll know me now, and so will you, whoever
you may be. This last account's for me.

It is! I write to hear the voice of Billy,
to watch the landscape quicken as I listen.
        "Make no mistake, Judge . . ." (Billy called me Judge
right from the start, and wouldn't be corrected.)
        "Judge, I'll tell you, never mind the gossip.
I liked that boy, and that boy liked me too,

"as good as anyone, though I'm a man
who should have died before he drew a breath.
That's what they'll tell you now that Mark is dead.
It took his death to make me out a devil;
they didn't talk that way before he died.
I did what I could do. I meant to save him.

"But you know what we had back then for traffic.
I had to go on foot, and it was hot,
and it was all uphill, a mile at least,
from way out there until I reached the flat,
and almost that again down to the tar.
If you could see me sweat! And my old heart,

"like a bagged hen! I wanted him to live,
but did his life mean Billy had to die?
I asked myself. They'd call that selfish, Judge,
but could they say what good it would have done
for both of us to go? Oh yes, I've heard:
'If Blainville had to up and lose the one,

"too bad it couldn't get shut of the other.'
As if the things that drove this town to hell
were all my doing. As if I was a wizard.
If I had died, would that young man come back?
Well, they believe it somehow. Never mind.
I had to stop for breath, and that was that.

199

"I lay against that twisty pasture pine
in Simpsons' field. (That tree is lively yet.
You wonder how many birds have rigged a nest
in all its boughs, how many spots of dew
and rain and snow have come to it and gone,
how many bugs have hidden in its bark.

"You wonder at those things. At least I do . . .)
I lay against the trunk and, looking up,
saw one of those big buzzards looking down.
We had them in those days, but they were rare,
so maybe I was dozing even then.
'I hope he'll let me die before he comes.'

"I said those words out loud, I think, as if
to say a thing out loud could make a spell.
I didn't want to die at all, you see.
I'd go in comfort anyway, I thought.
The sun was out of sight, or mostly, now.
Late summer afternoons! You know what I mean . . ."

        You know what I mean, said Billy, raising up
his crippled hand to mop away the sweat
his vision brought. Many times he said it:
"You know what I mean," he'd ask or state. I nodded.
        He carried on: "The first thing that I saw
when I woke up was that a star was out.

"And it was cool. I figured—I still do—
I stood as good a show as any neighbor
to get to paradise. Maybe I'd died!
That's what I thought. I even started looking
out for May. (She was the better half,
no doubt about it. She knew the bushes and flowers,

"she knew how much I missed the sheep and pastures.)
I watched a string of black duck settle in
on Wagner's beaver pond. A little weasel
was getting set for winter: already he wore
his high white socks. I heard that pretty thrush
you hear at dusk when there isn't any breeze.

200

"You see, I wasn't churchly, but I thought
if heaven's worth the breath the preachers use,
it'll be just like your life was at its best.
You've heard how people say, 'I pinched myself.'
By God, I did! To see if things would change.
When I sat up, that little weasel dove,

"but otherwise things looked about the same.
It brought back maybe half a dozen times
in life when things go on, but seem so right
you think they'll go forever with no harm.
The times I've had like that were at the farm,
when I'd be working hard all day, my mind

"hard on the job—whatever: digging, shearing—
and then I'd stop and turn, and everything
was in its place, and had a kind of shine.
You couldn't help but want to speak or sing.
Some kind of thanks, I guess. I'm not for church,
I said, but there you are.
                              I sat and watched

"the ridges. They kept swallowing the light,
all that white and yellow going blue.
I've always loved that business. I still do . . ."
        And Billy loved to talk, and as he wandered,
the hills took on the look that he described,
as if his words were sorcery,

as if the winter were summer, and moon were sun,
and far from being short, the Old Year's day
would last forever.
                    "There was, and I admit it,"
Billy said, "some bounce now in my toes.
A lot more than before, and I made time.
And not because poor Mark was in that hole.

"By Jesus, Judge, I'll say it! I felt good.
Is that what killed Mark dead? You know it isn't.
For all I know, the boy was long since gone.
But I went on until I came to Cammon's.

201

I knocked the door till Elsie finished peeking
through the curtains and finally opened up.

"I knew her all my life. I meant to speak,
for all the good it ever would have done.
Elsie liked to gab, but she had no phone,
no more than I did. I don't know too much,
but I know it takes a telephone right here
to ring another there. I meant to speak.

"Before I got a word in, though, she chirped,
'Nice evening, Billy.' Just what I was thinking . . .
Go on and live to be an older fool
than Billy, Judge. You'll never know the way
I mean that, and you'll likely curse me too.
She came out on the step. We turned around

"and watched the bullbats worrying the bugs.
We saw the moon hike overtop The Bald Man.
You see it from your house. You know the one?"
        How could Fields think this was information?
That mountain is the first thing that you see.
And yet when Billy named a thing for me,

I'd listen, as if hearing Revelation.
For forty years, The Bald Man's been the same.
The summer folks don't put their houses there!
Its giant granite dune commands the air,
and summer or winter, complements the moon
that wanders over it.
                    "We talked a spell

"in Elsie's rooms. We talked about the town
when we were young, the way it was back then—
pastures; fences; sheep. These scrubby woods
grew up when farmers couldn't make a go.
Their sons went to the city, or joined the army,
or shot their bolts out slaving with machines.

"We talked about all that before I told her
that Mark was lying out beneath her cow.
I haven't breathed a word about this, Judge,

though poor old Elsie Cammon died soon after,
and may God bless her! though she lied and said
she tried to move me on, but I was stubborn.

"Judge, she *smiled*. 'Billy, you ain't magic.'
That's the words she used. And that's the point.
It wasn't that I never meant to go
and raise some help. The better neighbor figures
all the walking played out Billy's mind.
But Judge, I'll tell you, I felt right as rain.

"We sat and drank another cup together,
and talked about the weather. Little things,
like people do. And when I thought of Mark
down in that grave, I thought for all of us
there comes a time, and maybe this is his.
And sat there happy, Judge, between us two,

"that it was his, not mine. Now that's all wrong,
because a man gets just so many years,
and I'd used up a better share of them
than Mark had done. And so I should have died
out by that tree, for that way Mark would live.
And that way, when his brothers came to fetch him,

"his blood would jump back in him from the ground,
and Elsie's cow would fly clean up to heaven,
and Elsie's fence would always be tight-strung,
and that choker apple never would have grown,
because old Fields had gone before his time,
and Blainville would be better than it was—

"the sheep would all come back and browse the hills,
the big old barns would still be up and plumb,
there'd be a foot of soil on every pasture,
and no one would go marching off to war,
and all our men and women would love forever . . ."
        I stopped him there. The old man's sweat was pouring

off his skin and down the tumbled bedclothes,
the way mine does sometimes.

But not tonight.
Tonight, recording this for you and you
—outsider, native, woman, man, or child—
but mostly for myself, as I've confessed,
I'll lie here with my story, cool, a while.

A little time, while the moon plays on The Bald Man,
I'll hold to it, and you can judge the rest.

Upcountry Speedway

Each of us strangely anxious   my daughter and I
driving here   in line   on this unseemly
road   nothing more than a logging trail
reclaimed   our windows down   though this is the final
evening   the last heroics   September already
already a chill from the glacier   Stars   How small
ahead   what we agree to call a roar
Second growth all but erases the babble
of revving race car engines   by local agreement
restricted to minimal power   six cylinders stock

Not of recent manufacture   All
will be buried in dust   Minuscule town and track
¼ mile on the outside lane   Young girlfriends
or wives cluster by village   Orient   Linneus
Wytopitlock   wide spots in the tarmac
We have our tickets   We hear the women cheer
men called Wayne or Brian   in suits emblazoned
with names   their own   their sweethearts'   sponsors'
Beauty's the female feature   frailest beauty
poised to cede itself to creases of worry

At money   fat   booze   an odd lump under
the Dacron   maybe a bruise   One prays   One swears
at her lover's rival   is joined   rebutted   insulted
Cheating's   the standard slander   Some men joke
waiting to race in the pits   Their children race
each other   boys and girls   down the grandstand
ramps or   older   betray themselves by screaming
abuse at the opposite sex or   older still
stroll toward trees   backseats   It's the final heat
Labor Day   *Gentlemen start your engines*

The official leans from his rickety tower   The green
flag flutters   At length our cries are lost
in the whine and protest of twenty badly used
autos careening toward the final turn
A few along the way appear to have broken
off the dirt   but no one ever gets hurt
So says a tiny grandma seated beside me
You can trust your car to the man who wears
the star stitched on her shirt   Her words are part
reassurance   it seems   and part lament

How few are satisfied   The factions shriek
dissatisfaction at the Nova that orbits
the circuit half-speed   trailing the checkered pennant
of the victor   Women   bitter   gather belongings
Wrecks are hauled away   We follow the throng
Beside us   up on a father's shoulders   a child
of uncertain gender calls out   the ancient tease
No one can get me   My own child's breaths are mist
against the mountain   under the chilly heavens
They mingle with exhalations from dark coupés

Spite: Her Tale

Someone else would tell a different version:

There was a tree, a twisty beech, out back,
no earthly use, not even for a shade.
You know the way of a tree in this cold place:
it starts a hefty trunk, and then the winds
and winters grind at it, the tightwad earth
will starve it till it almost seems to send
branches sideways-out to look for friends.

I recollect that beech's early years:

Mighty plans, just as I said, to start,
which it would drop in time . . . but first it tried
somehow to sneak its way to being tall:
at three feet high, it took a funny swerve,
headed south a year or two, and then
came back in line to make a loop, or bow.
After that, it grew just anyhow.

Where it curved, it left a sort of seat.

I've made a loop myself. I'll start again.
My Harry's lights went out about when mine did.
I never saw them lay him down, just heard
the diggers grunt, the clods and gravel tumble,
the frost-clumps fall in too, the frozen sods.
Then came the spring, so quick you thought it couldn't.
Our Buck got done with school and married Susan,

and she moved here to run the farm with him.

We say The Farm, though Harry didn't die
the way I guess he should have—flinging hay,
or pulling calves, or mucking out a stall.
He fell among old tire irons and ratchets,
his cutting torch on fire, a snakey tailpipe
hung at him from a Ford up on the hoist,
the muffler shop's blue fumes too much at last.

His heart was never what it should have been.

Buck claims he's added two head to the herd.
I know better. I can hear the truth.
And after all, I lived here all those years
with both my eyes. I never say a thing.
He works a night job, cleaning up a morgue.
Not that I judge—a farmer nowadays
does what he must to help the farm get by.

What I want to talk about is spite:

or maybe I should call it cruelty.
It doesn't matter anyway. Just words.
Now understand me. I'm not out for pity.
No one ever hit me or abused me,
though I've got just enough imagination
to picture it, the old man coming home,
a half a case in him, and feeling down.

Bad pay and bills . . . but she's the one to suffer,

to get beat up for nothing that she's done.
Thing is, I think I know how *he* feels too;
the world's a funny place, make no mistake.
Buck and Sue would likely tell this different,
but even I don't say the word *abused*.
Back to the tree . . . but first let me confess
that at the start I fairly was a mess:

I moped and whined, a lot more than I should have,

but I'd been never one to stand around
with people waiting on me—I could do it!—

and never thought how much I used my eyes,
how much I'd taken pleasure from my sight.
(You know the saying: "You don't miss your water . . .")
Don't get me wrong: I don't mean watching things
they dream make women purr in magazines—

rising dough, the patterns in a quilt.

If I looked at such stuff, I had plain reasons:
a person has to feed and warm herself.
When I say sight, I mean a person's hands—
the way they'll spread or clamp or pick or fiddle;
or, when you look straight into it, a face—
its grins, its grimaces and in-betweens.
A cloud. A track. A brook. A mink. A tree.

I liked a busyness that wanted eyes,

just like poor Harry: how it sickens me
to think he spent his last years tinkering
and twisting screws. He wasn't made for that.
I had to dig down somewhere for a will;
I had to figure I could sit and rot,
and wreck the children's lives into the bargain,
or I could somehow, someway get a move on.

And so I did. I learned to watch with ears.

It's not that I saw much, but what I saw
I saw as clear as any sighted person.
I think that once I started it came easy
because, when I'd had eyes, I'd kept an eye out . . .
But let me get back to that twisty tree,
the one thing that I came to know the best,
the thing that helped me locate all the rest.

Every day, no matter what the weather,

I'd get myself out to it, settle in,
my backside and my back a perfect fit
inside the bow or loop I've spoken of.
I wore that cranny's bark smooth where I sat,
and where I laid my hands was smooth as well.

I saw things when the beech would creak with wind,
or even when an owl came to a limb.

In peace or torment, I could see the tree.
When squirrels squabbled on a higher branch,
when nuts plopped on the ground, if there were nuts,
when winter redpolls, siskins, chickadees
would come or go, or leather-colored leaves
that hang tight through the snows would flap and click:
I'd mark the sound and piece the tree together
(for all I know I got it wrong. I never

paid that beech much mind till I was blind).

And once I fitted out the shape again,
then I could see the farm; and once I saw
the farm, the cows or steers or calves, whatever,
then I felt I knew where I belonged
in all this universe . . . and all because
I'd noticed squirrels, leaves, a breeze, a bird.
All because I saw what I had heard,

and thought, and listened hard to what I thought.

In fact I came to see the tree much better
than even I saw Harry in my mind;
in fact I came to think of it as Harry,
a funny thing—there wasn't any reason:
I can't recall him speak of it at all
when he was living. It's the way I said:
it didn't even make a decent shade.

I never spoke a word about all this,

no solitary word to Buck or Susan
on what the tree's idea had come to mean—
not as you might guess that I was scared
they'd laugh at me for loving some old beech.
I wasn't sure for one thing it was love,
at least not for the tree. I couldn't say
just what it was. And so I didn't say.

But I had changed. There wasn't any doubt.

You know, it seemed that Buck and Sue preferred
when I was ugly—quick to snap, or cry.
Some people like you better broken down;
then all they think they have to do is tinker
with you like a gear. But understand:
I'm no philosopher; I'm not inclined.
I'll let you explain, if you've a mind,

the way they acted. Here it is, I think:

right before my eyes, they cut that tree
and sawed it up for cordwood. Now that's spite!
You can't just chop away a thing like that.
They claimed that all its branches had gone dead,
but I of course knew better, knew that tree
as well as my own soul, and I still do.
Did they mean for me to have no place to go?

Here it is. I keep it right inside.

It's hard to say what they keep. Cruelty—
I never feel a craving to return it.
They won't have any kids, although God knows
I don't claim that's the last bad fate God dreamed.
I had a child, and where did I come out?
I came out sitting up a tree, they'd say.
I know—they don't—just what that means to me.

Buck cleans dead men's dust from dark till dawn.

I stay alone on weekend nights. They dance
down in a place so full of lights it blinds,
or so they say (and turn their laughter mean)—
a place that blinds, a band that plays so loud
they can't hear what they say or even think.
I know the things I know. I nod and rock.
I never feel the need to pay them back.

Road Agent

When the sun rises, they get them away
and lie down in their dens.
Man goes forth to his work
and to his labor until the evening.
　　—Psalm 104

It doesn't seem so cursed in summer.
If a job could ever turn sweet, that's when.
There's just a little brush to tend.
Or I cuff the washboard flat with the grader.

You don't even have to swat the flies.
Diesel smoke and noise will drive them.
The best is, I can look to the mountain!
The seat will raise a man that high.

The plow's high, too, but you can't look off.
Sunup to sundown, eyes on the road.
The mountain's still there when it goes cold.
But in winter you have to mind yourself.

Your help will quit you sure as Judas.
I clear the ice and snow on my own.
Everyone seems to go to den.
Kiss them good-bye when the weather freezes.

They call on the town or move to the city.
It's soft, but it isn't by Jesus my way.
I'm not like the state boys out on the highway.
I don't despise what isn't easy.

I'm what I was made, and nothing else.
I mean to earn my bread by sweat.
Foolish, the things that some expect.
God helps them that help themselves.

Some can't dream why I'd keep at it.
No matter what this one and that one say.
They vote me back on town meeting day.
But the new folks' notions and mine are different.

(The oldtimers don't much like to talk.
I do it for them—I'm elected.
It comes with the work, and I guess it's expected.)
The newcomers squawk and I squawk back.

First thing to do, they say, is the schoolyard.
They have to get at the books, those kids!
(True, it's what my mother said.
The times would pass me by, she figured.)

But someone should bless the poor in school.
Everyone better not turn out bright.
They do, and these roads close down tonight.
They could own the world and lose their souls.

That's in a book, and makes some sense.
I graduated with less than I brought.
Of course I started going with Hat.
You couldn't call it a total loss.

We've kept on going, with six good children.
Say *that* for some that study college.
Say they got *that* out of all their knowledge.
Say they got it from education.

Last week I was working Sutter's Knoll.
I came on poor young Mrs. Grayson.
She had this little flimsy dress on.
You'd judge she was out for a summer stroll.

Her husband's diplomas would fill a trunk.
(Half-bare, she was, in a foot of snow!

I pretended a wing was loose on the plow.)
He's one of those jacket-and-necktie drunks.

Town Hall's the next that's got to be done.
The politicians insist on that.
They're damned important, you can bet.
I guess I oughtn't to run them down.

They hang on tougher than lots of others.
Take what few are left in The Grange.
It seems so quick, the way it's changed!
There aren't that many around to remember.

Things were different here one time.
The Grange is ready to fall on the ground.
Who cares nowadays in town?
I do it early, all the same.

Let them fire me: I've lived through worse.
It wasn't Happily-Ever-After.
It wasn't Everyone-Love-Your-Neighbor.
And the good Lord knows the money was scarce.

Then I plow the American Legion Post.
(There was always a battle or two somewhere.)
Schooling, politics, and war.
Father, Son, and Holy Ghost.

I'm not even supposed to do the church.
That road is twisty, even in light.
I wait and fuss with it in the night.
Taxpayer money—they'd moan and bitch.

Dead last, this house of God out here.
But He says from the mountain, The last will be first.
In the end He says, The first'll be last.
This is the one I fight to get clear.

The hardest one, in the cold of the year.

In memory of Roger Noyes

Private Boys' School, 3rd Grade

Teacher is like every woman, of course—
A "Mrs." Lives in a storybook house
Of whitest clapboard. Dick and Jane and Spot

Her dog will greet her after school gets out.
That's our joke. We see them all on a lawn
Of unspoiled grass, each shrub well planned, well pruned.

Soon she puts her satchel down in the hall
And does her rounds: fills up Spot's dish with meal,
Makes Janie's doll as neat as new again.

Maybe Dick is a less-than-perfect son,
Scolded like us for failed marks and manners.
"Wash up," she chides, then has him add figures

On paper clean as we can only dream.
Or so we hope, while Mr. Grady beams
Satisfaction at the roast in gravy,

Centered in the oven. Mrs. Grady
Strikes a match at last and holds it over
Every candle, tiny flame that hovers,

A momentary but punctilious dot
Above each flawless i. She may or not
Wear a ring, a thing outside our notice.

Once, a fearful downpour comes upon us,
Unlike the placid weathers in our books,
And as she herds us, slickered, to the bus,

The wind upfurls our Mrs. Grady's dress.
We glimpse rent stockings, rolled beneath blue knees;
Some wiseguy says, sophisticatedly,

"See Mrs. Grady's runs!" But she can't hear.
And then the cold, the gloomy time of year—
Light gets slight, and labor more obnoxious:

Subordinates, qualifiers, commas.
Even more sternness in the way we're taught;
She says strange things like, "Every sentence ought

To hold together now. Your stories have
To be real stories, rounded out, like life."
How we grimace, our tongues between our teeth,

At noun and predicate that won't agree,
At run-on phrase, question mark forgotten.
All our story notions come up rotten.

Term snaps shut. She claps us to her bosom,
Hotly, each in turn. She makes us kiss her,
Whimper, scarlet-eared, how much we'll miss her,

Though there's not one who doesn't feel distaste,
If only at her tear-bespattered face:
Has she not spent these months upbraiding us

Like ornery dogs for smears and tears and blots,
For "sloppiness," which showed we "planned badly"?
"These can spoil your lives," said Mrs. Grady.

Black Bear Cuffing for Food

After the leaf lookers' season, I'm alone
on the road to watch his labor.
      Time of the spendthrift maple,
      frost-burned fern,
      ripe riverside butternuts splashing
      into the water and gone.

Time by God to get set,
as he appears already to have learned,
      dark shoulders, rhythmic, heaving
      back and forth, back and forth,
      and in the rests,
      hand to mouth, hand to mouth.

He looks a little like Mongo Santamaria
rapt above the dried hide of his conga,
      thumping out "Watermelon Man,"
      memory I wrest
      from some gone nightclub cellar,
      thick with a general gray smoke.

Now halfway down
the hills in the dusk air's chill,
      it's cloud that is gray and thick.
      A wonder, the mind's autonomy—
      or enslavement . . . I smile to recall Mongo's drum,
      and over its crackle and pop the horns' glissandi.

I play them back in mind, alone
at the edge of Macalister's field,
      where a young bear cuffs for ants in latest October.

The work is for scant return
and however furious, slow.
Soon sleep, at whose muddy far end will be hunger.

I mean for all these signs to mean:
I imagine how, come spring, a rusty stalk,
      missed in the reaping,
      will show here and there in the rows;
      and a scrap of someone's shirttail or frock,
      on barbed wire next to the lane.

For now, the bear is disappearing
into the twilight and fog,
      into the time
      of glowing jack-o'-lanterns without measure
      beneath the colored corn that hangs in windows.
      Now children study the rags they'll turn into costumes.

And I, who've merely ridden to the grocery store,
will start again
      back through woods in their final flames.
      Past the pond where sometimes for pleasure
      I flick a bright fly for fish I let go,
      and down the neat gravel drive, beyond the door,

      my family waits. It's suppertime.
      Down in the islands bright melons are a staple.
      How exotic it seems, and oh,
      and oh how colorful . . .

In the Blind

For Tommy White, my oldest friend

As in water face answers to face, the Proverb says,
so the mind of man reflects the man . . .
which must in my case mean the surface is roiled
as this one before me when it's lashed by furious beavers.
What a lot of time I spend in the blind,
splashing from thought to thought,
moving at random.
And how often I reach for you,
we shared so much, we rode all over God's acre
together, and always thought the same.
Now that we shoot toward fifty,

what does it all add up to?
Quick birds that breast the sun and rob my breath;
the revelation of internal pattern
in a fireplace log
at the moment my ax lays it open,
before I throw it on the heap
to dry, to be burned. Whiffs of memory.
Is the beautiful random enough?
Everything that is here and must go away.
(I wonder if you have time
for all this stuff.)

Sometimes late in November,
the river will suddenly turn austere, abstract,
as if its waves would cease their movement, stiffen.
Maybe you remember
how we used to argue over religion.

Especially in the fall,
it seems I still expend a lot of my life
waiting for something to light beside me and stay.
How often I'll be here,
the marsh alive around me
—something that riffles the slough, a rustle in weeds—

but the sky so empty only thought can fill it.
Except for the slow-motion stars. And except for Queen Moon:
just this morning, perfectly round,
she still was high, and my thought was of you
one time when you offered me a confession,
and it was hard,
for we thought of ourselves as rock-hard adolescents.
"Sometimes," you said, "I could cry
when I hear that Christmas carol,
'O Little Town of Bethlehem.'"

I laughed. I know exactly what you mean,
though we don't anymore have much in common
except this past that speaks to us in symbols
—the important part, at least—
and usually mutely.
It's that part about the deep and dreamless sleep,
am I right?
That, and the way the silent stars go by.
I think I knew even then what I feel now,
however hard of expression.
This morning, I say, the moon was full,

and there I was, half-asleep,
in my ignorance waiting for some wondrous declension,
the advent of . . . what?
There are moments in the blind
when I could simply lay back my head and bellow.
Do you remember those summer evenings
in your father's Rocket 88
when we'd fly back and forth like swallows
trapped in a building?

Here to there to there to here!
And yet we felt ourselves free,

the radio loud, loudly singing along.
Remember the Dells' old anthem?
"O, What a Night."
We didn't know where we were going,
but everything on the way was so perfectly lovely
—the silent little towns winking like planets,
the rolling frost-studded country—
moment to moment to moment,
what could it matter?
Over the undulant doo-wop, that falsetto.
Something also that hovered above us,

at least we thought so.
Some ever-available charm. I yet can see,
as if they were caught in a mirror,
our heads thrown back in song,
eyes to the sky,
improvising harmony, light like a symbol
of something up there, sure and answerable.
Possible, undivided, great.
As if we were not moving at all.
Streaming down on each kindred face,
a light like grace.

Wedding Anniversary

For M.R.B.

Even past sunrise, frog legions peeped in spring
where—as if for him—the creek jagged near.
And yet from dawn, from spring, something was missing.
There were quartzes and pyrites and schists and mica plates
on the opposite scarp. They'd crackle. He would stir
the back pool's gathered algae with a stick
till the world spun in a vortex that contained
lights, quicksilver minnows, verdigris newts.
And after, reflected riverside trees would shiver,
their birds odd lapidary fruit that sang.
His awkward schoolroom recitations seemed
an age away. And yet there was something missing.

The stars above the pastures of adolescence
were profligate, scattered; and all the whispered words
he traded with his friends, though banal, thrilled him.
It was as if rich adulthood would take
the form of speech, as if to talk enough
to companions would be to lisp his way to treasure,
various as those stars, or the sighs and chippings
of amorous insects, nightbirds, rodents, cattle,
or summer timothy stalks, or breezes panting
warmly. He recalls how their radio crooned
"Shangri-la," "Rags to Riches," whatever.
Rifeness was all. But there was an absence too.

Later he learned the words, the syntax, moods
of another language. Still later he found himself

high in the Pyrenees, unsponsored, free.
He had no cash, but could speak and charm no less
than *Monsieur le maire*, who accepted his draft and poured
coin from the hamlet's coffers and poured him wine.
They leaned out over a rail to see September's
shatter of water on rocks in the gorge below.
Then mayor and manchild stumbled house to house—
he remembers the musical speeches of introduction,
as if the boy himself were somehow a treasure.
Copious tears at parting, then something missing

All through the long, olfactory ramble north:
meadow-scent, soft coal, diesel's perfumes,
sawdust-and-urine whiff in the tiny *relais*,
Gauloises, cheroots, and, once in Paris, cassis.
Liquor-courageous, he nodded to the lady.
And then, upstairs, the spirits fading, he bellowed,
to mask his shyness, "I have had enough!"
"*J'en ai marre!*" To which she replied, "*De quoi?*"
Mute, he handed over what money was left
from the mayor's store, and mortified waited outside
on the balcony, its grillwork broken by light.
He thought, "*De quoi?*" Exactly. Enough of what?

Trout, platooned and hungry in western Montana,
the gilded browns, the rainbows more than rainbows,
the cutthroats' cheek-plates crimson as any wound:
breaking the flawless surface, flawless themselves,
they arched their backs and sipped his little fly
with its tinsel and feather, never so lovely as they were.
Coyotes sang the sun to splendid disaster.
It fell on the rim of the mesa, imploding in flame,
across which flew the tuneful, crop-full geese
while black hawks wheeled, while great bull elk came forth
to bugle challenge, courtship down the buttes,
which shone like mercury now. And something missing,

Something that failed as well to show from ice
outside his house, New Hampshire. Within, soft groans
from his ancient timbers. His clothing snapped with static.
One songless nuthatch lit to taste his feeder.
It seemed that nature vanished into mind,
that pool and pasture, mountain and minnow, frogs,
odors, effects of touch and sound and light
had each become mere object of recall.
The newest New Year passed and seemed not new,
but raced to retrospection, as would spring
and summer and autumn, so he thought, like winter
missing something. How could he know you

would come, and come the day of which he sings?
Has gone on singing. Will go on to sing.

Illinois Poetry Series

Laurence Lieberman, Editor

History Is Your Own Heartbeat
Michael S. Harper (1971)

The Foreclosure
Richard Emil Braun (1972)

The Scrawny Sonnets and Other
Narratives
Robert Bagg (1973)

The Creation Frame
Phyllis Thompson (1973)

To All Appearances: Poems New and
Selected
Josephine Miles (1974)

The Black Hawk Songs
Michael Borich (1975)

Nightmare Begins Responsibility
Michael S. Harper (1975)

The Wichita Poems
Michael Van Walleghen (1975)

Images of Kin: New and Selected Poems
Michael S. Harper (1977)

Poems of the Two Worlds
Frederick Morgan (1977)

Cumberland Station
Dave Smith (1977)

Tracking
Virginia R. Terris (1977)

Riversongs
Michael Anania (1978)

On Earth as It Is
Dan Masterson (1978)

Coming to Terms
Josephine Miles (1979)

Death Mother and Other Poems
Frederick Morgan (1979)

Goshawk, Antelope
Dave Smith (1979)

Local Men
James Whitehead (1979)

Searching the Drowned Man
Sydney Lea (1980)

With Akhmatova at the Black Gates
Stephen Berg (1981)

Dream Flights
Dave Smith (1981)

More Trouble with the Obvious
Michael Van Walleghen (1981)

The American Book of the Dead
Jim Barnes (1982)

The Floating Candles
Sydney Lea (1982)

Northbook
Frederick Morgan (1982)

Collected Poems, 1930–83
Josephine Miles (1983)

The River Painter
Emily Grosholz (1984)

Healing Song for the Inner Ear
Michael S. Harper (1984)

The Passion of the Right-Angled Man
T. R. Hummer (1984)

Dear John, Dear Coltrane
Michael S. Harper (1985)

Poems from the Sangamon
John Knoepfle (1985)

In It
Stephen Berg (1986)

The Ghosts of Who We Were
Phyllis Thompson (1986)

Moon in a Mason Jar
Robert Wrigley (1986)

Lower-Class Heresy
T. R. Hummer (1987)

Poems: New and Selected
Frederick Morgan (1987)

Furnace Harbor: A Rhapsody of the
North Country
Philip D. Church (1988)

Bad Girl, with Hawk
Nance Van Winckel (1988)

Blue Tango
Michael Van Walleghen (1989)

Eden
Dennis Schmitz (1989)

Waiting for Poppa at the Smithtown
Diner
Peter Serchuk (1990)

Great Blue
Brendan Galvin (1990)

What My Father Believed
Robert Wrigley (1991)

Something Grazes Our Hair
S. J. Marks (1991)

Walking the Blind Dog
G. E. Murray (1992)

The Sawdust War
Jim Barnes (1992)

The God of Indeterminacy
Sandra McPherson (1993)

Off-Season at the Edge of the World
Debora Greger (1994)

Counting the Black Angels
Len Roberts (1994)

Oblivion
Stephen Berg (1995)

To Us, All Flowers Are Roses
Lorna Goodison (1995)

Honorable Amendments
Michael S. Harper (1995)

Points of Departure
Miller Williams (1995)

Dance Script with Electric Ballerina
Alice Fulton (reissue, 1996)

To the Bone: New and Selected Poems
Sydney Lea (1996)

Floating on Solitude
Dave Smith (3-volume reissue, 1996)

Bruised Paradise
Kevin Stein (1996)

Walt Whitman Bathing
David Wagoner (1996)

National Poetry Series

Eroding Witness
Nathaniel Mackey (1985)
Selected by Michael S. Harper

Palladium
Alice Fulton (1986)
Selected by Mark Strand

Cities in Motion
Sylvia Moss (1987)
Selected by Derek Walcott

The Hand of God and a Few
Bright Flowers
William Olsen (1988)
Selected by David Wagoner

The Great Bird of Love
Paul Zimmer (1989)
Selected by William Stafford

Stubborn
Roland Flint (1990)
Selected by Dave Smith

The Surface
Laura Mullen (1991)
Selected by C. K. Williams

The Dig
Lynn Emanuel (1992)
Selected by Gerald Stern

My Alexandria
Mark Doty (1993)
Selected by Philip Levine

The High Road to Taos
Martin Edmunds (1994)
Selected by Donald Hall

Theater of Animals
Samn Stockwell (1995)
Selected by Louise Glück

The Broken World
Marcus Cafagña (1996)
Selected by Yusef Komunyakaa

New and Selected Poems, 1962–92
Laurence Lieberman (1993)

The Dig and *Hotel Fiesta*
Lynn Emanuel (1994)

For a Living: The Poetry of Work
Edited by Nicholas Coles and Peter Oresick (1995)

The Tracks We Leave: Poems on Endangered Wildlife of North America (1996)
Barbara Helfgott Hyett

Other Poetry Volumes

Local Men and *Domains*
James Whitehead (1987)

Her Soul beneath the Bone: Women's Poetry on Breast Cancer
Edited by Leatrice Lifshitz (1988)

Days from a Dream Almanac
Dennis Tedlock (1990)

Working Classics: Poems on Industrial Life
Edited by Peter Oresick and Nicholas Coles (1990)

Hummers, Knucklers, and Slow Curves: Contemporary Baseball Poems
Edited by Don Johnson (1991)

The Double Reckoning of Christopher Columbus
Barbara Helfgott Hyett (1992)

Selected Poems
Jean Garrigue (1992)